The Communist Manifesto

Crofts Classics

GENERAL EDITORS

Samuel H. Beer, *Harvard University*

O. B. Hardison, Jr., *The Folger Shakespeare Library*

KARL MARX and
FRIEDRICH ENGELS

The Communist Manifesto

with selections from
*The Eighteenth Brumaire of
Louis Bonaparte* and *Capital*

by KARL MARX

EDITED BY

Samuel H. Beer

HARVARD UNIVERSITY

AHM Publishing Corporation
Arlington Heights, Illinois 60004

ISBN: 0-88295-055-X
(Formerly 0-390-22909-1)

-

Library of Congress Card Number: 55-10808

PRINTED IN THE UNITED STATES OF AMERICA
787
Thirty-sixth Printing

CONTENTS

CONTENTS

INTRODUCTION

MARXISM, it is often said, is a secular religion. That term, strictly speaking, is self-contradictory. A religion, in the usual meaning of the word, involves a belief in some timeless, and therefore nonsecular, dimension. Yet there are good reasons for using the word to describe the Marxist system. If, as students of society, we are to find parallels to this system and its effect on men, we are obliged to fall back on analogies with religion. Like a religion it is at once a theory of the world and a program of action. As a theory it is comprehensive, comprising doctrines touching every important aspect of individual and social existence. It includes a theory of economics, sociology, politics, and ethics; attempts have been made to give it a bearing upon the various spheres of natural science. As a program of action, it has shown a capacity to inspire the fanatical loyalty and rigid discipline of patriotism, but unlike patriotism and like religion, it has swept over national boundaries as the creed of a world-wide movement.

Marxism is especially like religion in the nature of certain basic questions which it attempts to answer. It includes—though not under these names—a theory of how evil came into the world and how it will be eliminated; a vision of powers which are beyond man's control and inflict suffering upon him, but which carry him onward to a blessed fulfillment; a prophecy of a final paradise where humanity will live in perfect freedom and happiness. It is impossible to understand the deep appeal of the Marxist system unless we consider its powerful effect upon emotions which are essentially religious.

As a whole, the Marxist system is prophecy founded upon vision. But it can and ought also to be considered on its intellectual merits. Its assertions can be tested by the

vii

usual canons of evidence and logic. The appeal to internal consistency and, especially, to the facts of history can settle the question of the validity of its theories of sociology, economics, and politics. These deserve serious consideration and should not be rejected simply out of moral disapproval or because Communists, who accept them, are an evil influence in the world today. Often, within the exaggeration of Marxist doctrine, a kernel of truth may be found. The Marxist system of thought is particularly useful, however, because it raises questions which force the reader to state his own beliefs—or doubts—on important subjects. We may, for instance, reject the extreme economic determinism of the Marxist theory, but we need to think out our own position on the possible relations between economic development and other aspects of society. For the person who believes in the power of conscience and moral ideals and in the capacity of the human mind to understand and control society, there is no better exercise than matching his beliefs against the challenging dogmas of Marxism.

To reduce Marxism to a single, coherent body of thought is far from an easy task. The term refers not only to the views of the two inseparable collaborators, Marx and Engels, whose ideas quite naturally changed and developed from one work to another. It also includes the interpretations and restatements of these views by the host of disciples who have acclaimed the system in the past hundred years or so. Even if we were to try to confine our discussion to the doctrines of self-proclaimed Marxists in the world today we should have a wide variety of views to recount: not only those of the Communists of Soviet Russia, Western Europe, and China, but also the quite different, though still allegedly Marxist ideas, of anti-Communists such as the Social Democrats of Germany, the socialists of France, and the leftwing Laborites of Britain. Quite sufficient is the effort to state in broad outline what may be called the Marxism of Marx; that is, certain of the main doctrines which he (and Engels) elaborated in their principal works. These are not by any means unambiguously clear, and the reader is encouraged to use this Introduction merely as a starting point from which to conduct his own study and criticism of what Marx and Marxists have written.

I

THE THEORY OF OBJECTIVE DEVELOPMENT

The Marxist system has many branches. The central doctrine, however, is the conception which came to be known as Historical Materialism, or the materialist conception of history. The classic formulation of this doctrine is found in the preface to the *Critique of Political Economy* which Marx published in 1859. There he describes how he was led to "the conclusion that legal relations as well as forms of the state could neither be understood by themselves, nor explained by the so-called general progress of the human mind, but that they are rooted in the material conditions of life." Expanding on this statement, he continued:

In the social production of their material life, men enter into definite relations that are indispensable and independent of their wills; these relations of production correspond to a definite state of the development of their material forces of production.

The sum total of these relations of production makes up the economic structure of society—the real foundation on which arises a legal and political superstructure and to which correspond definite forms of social consciousness.

The mode of production of material life determines the social, political and intellectual life process in general. It is not the consciousness of men that determines their existence, but rather it is their social existence that determines their consciousness.

At a certain stage of their development, the material forces of production in society come into conflict with the existing relations of production or—what is but a legal expression of the same thing—with the property relations within which they have been at work before. From forms of development of the productive forces, these relations turn into their fetters. Then begins an epoch of social revolution. With the change of the economic foundation, the entire immense superstructure is more or less rapidly transformed.

Three essentials of the Marxist conception of history are involved in this statement: (1) That the economic structure of society—in the precommunist period—is not and cannot be deliberately planned and controlled, but develops independently of human will and thought and according to objective social law; (2) That this developing economic structure determines what takes place in other spheres of social life, such as class structure, the state, law, religion and ethics; (3) That the course of history is inevitably punctuated by violent revolutions, each marking the transition to a more advanced stage of historical development.

Equally important, although not suggested in the passage quoted above, is a fourth idea: that men shall surely be delivered from their slavery to one another and to historical necessity when in the fullness of time the proletarian revolution ushers in the communist society. In what follows we shall consider these four essentials of Marxism, beginning with the problem of objective development.

How can the economic structure—which Marx also refers to as the relations of production and as the mode of production—develop except through the ideas and motives of men? When goods are bought and sold, when factories are built or fields cultivated, conscious decisions and purposes lie behind these events. As Marx himself emphasizes, when a human being makes something—for instance, a house—the thing exists first as a plan or image in his mind before it is constructed in material reality.[1] Quite different are the changes of physical nature. The processes of geology, for instance, take place without being planned or intended or directed by a mind. How

[1] "We have to consider labor in a form peculiar to the human species . . . many a human architect is put to shame by the skill with which a bee constructs her cell. But what from the very first distinguishes the most incompetent architect from the best of bees, is that the architect has built a cell in his head before he constructs it in wax. The labor process ends in the creation of something which, when the process began, already existed in the worker's imagination . . ." *Capital* (Everyman edn., London, 1930), pp. 169-170.

can one hold, as Marx does, on the one hand that men are conscious, purposive, and indeed inventive, and on the other hand, that their social life, like the processes of blind, physical nature, develops independently of their thought and will?

Thanks not a little to the influence of Marx, this paradox is today a commonplace of social science, which is very much concerned with studying what may be called objective development in society. Economists interest themselves, for instance, in working out the unintended consequences of the behavior of a number of people buying and selling in a free market. In such a situation, each individual is continually making decisions such as whether he shall or shall not offer his goods and what prices he shall ask for them. Yet the final outcome of the "higgling" of the market is not planned and very likely not even foreseen by anyone. So with the other processes of a free, competitive economy: while on the one hand they are carried on by inventive, calculating human beings, on the other hand they arrive at results which no mind has previously conceived and purposively carried out. It is as if, to use Adam Smith's phrase, these processes were guided by "an invisible hand."

Not only in economics, but also in other spheres, processes of objective development take place, providing a subject-matter in which the social scientist seeks to discover uniformities or "laws" of social change and causation. To accept this general conclusion one need not be a Marxist. Nor is there anything peculiarly Marxist about its application to the study of long-run historical development, although Marx was concerned less with repetitive and short-run processes—such as price formation in a free market—than with the long-run tendencies of economic development.

What then distinguishes the Marxian theory of objective development from the notion of objective development in general? Economic development, according to Marx, is subject to certain inexorable laws and must pass through certain definite stages. Each stage has its distinctive mode of production, its system by which the means of production—that is, tools, land, materials, etc.—are controlled and by which labor is applied to production. The earliest stage was that of primitive communism and the final stage —yet to come—will be again communist. In between, Marx distinguished three modes of production, each based on private property in the means of production: the slave system of ancient Rome and Greece, the feudal system, and the modern capitalist system. In each, the mode of production was determined by the forces of production; as these forces developed, they reached a point at which they came into conflict with the mode of production; out of this conflict—marked in the social superstructure by intense class war and political revolution—emerged a new and more advanced mode of production.

This process of objective economic development Marx referred to as a "dialectical process" and we shall not get at his distinctive view of history unless we examine what he meant by this phrase. The notion of a dialectical process Marx took over from the philosophy of Hegel [2] and for Marx as for Hegel such a process has three phases. A "thesis" produces an entity opposed to it, the "anti-thesis"; the conflict between these two results in a "synthesis," which unites the two opposing entities in a higher unity and itself becomes a "thesis" setting in motion a new stage of the dialectical process. For Hegel this was the pattern in which thought developed—an initial statement of truth giving rise to an opposing statement, from which opposition a more comprehensive notion emerged including both partial truths. Furthermore, for Hegel, since in his view the development of thought governed history, history itself followed a dialectical pattern.

While rejecting with supreme scorn the view that it is thought which governs history, Marx, nevertheless, took over from Hegel the concept of a dialectical process, deriving from it his basic laws of objective social development. The existing mode of production in a particular stage of

[2] **George Wilhelm Friedrich Hegel** (1770-1831), German philosopher, from 1818 until his death professor at the University of Berlin where he founded a school of thought which profoundly affected Marx after he came to study there in 1836.

history he referred to as the "thesis," the opposing productive forces which emerge within it as the "antithesis," while the new and more productive economy which results from the union of the two he termed the "synthesis." Marxist economic history, therefore, like the progress of Hegelian truth, is governed by the laws of dialectical movement. Under these laws the mode of production is a whole, a real unity, which gradually produces the forces which will transform it in a sudden catastrophe. The principal motor of development is not thought, but on the contrary, the "productive forces" of the economy.

What did Marx mean by "productive forces?" The briefest way of putting it is to say that they are the elements of which the mode of production is composed; they are the parts, it is the whole. In a modern economy, they would include, for instance, tools, machines, and factories; the materials and natural resources which enter into production; the work of labor, skilled, unskilled, and technical; the manner—e.g. the assembly line—in which labor is used and, in general, the techniques by which production is carried on.

In the development of these parts—in their isolated and unorganized development—objective economic development takes place. Human thought and will enter into this process, but to a limited degree. When the productive forces are increased by the introduction of an invention—for instance, Watt's steam engine—it is obvious that the inventor planned his new machine, tool, or technique. He will not intend or be able to foresee, however, many of the consequences of introducing this machine—for instance, "the dark Satanic mills" which resulted from the introduction of the steam engine in the early days of the Industrial Revolution.

Nor are inventions and new techniques generally the principal means by which productive forces grow. They are only one, and before modern times, one of the least important means. The transition from slave society to feudal society and from feudal society to capitalist society, according to Marx, was accomplished without major advances in technology. The Marxist system lays stress or the fact that without any new departure in thought, such as invention involves, the simple addition of familiar elements may expand productive powers and even result in considerable changes in the pattern of the production process itself.

The underlying process appears to be gradual—a slow, step-by-step growth in the productive forces of the economy. But gradualism, economic or political, is not the theme of the Marxist system which conceives of history as advancing through vast and catastrophic transitions when the productive forces come into conflict with the mode of production. But how in the name of common sense are we to conceive of such a conflict? The productive forces, as we have seen, are to be understood as the constituent parts of the economic system. The mode of production, on the other hand, is the whole system constituted by these parts, taken, not as isolated elements, but as interdependent with one another in the production process of the economy.

Interdependence we can readily understand. But Marx means more than interdependence. He means, as he says, that "the production relations of every society form a whole." [3] How can the parts (the productive forces) form a whole (the mode of production) and yet come into conflict with the whole? If we were thinking of human ideas of the mode of production, the problem would not be difficult. We can suppose that people might have, on the one hand, an idea of the economic system and, on the other, separate ideas of its parts. We can readily imagine furthermore that their ideas of the parts might, for some reason or other, become incompatible with their idea of the whole. Marx, however, is not talking about human ideas, but about an objective economic system. Certainly he does not mean there is some sort of vast "social mind" which is above the individuals and in which this idea of the whole can exist separately from the ideas of the parts. Can he mean there is some "social purpose," some historical *telos* which is the means or the forum of this conflict? Either supposition would be hard to reconcile with what we normally consider to be a materialist view of the

[3] *The Poverty of Philosophy* (New York, 1936), p. 93

world. At this point of our analysis of Marx, we come upon
the intimation of entities and powers which transcend the
world of every-day experience.

For Marx, change within each period is gradual, but at
the transitional point it becomes catastrophic. Changes in
quantity, say the Marxists, become a change in quality. As
a result of the accretion of small quantitative changes in
its constituent parts, the economic system changes *as a
whole*. And corresponding to this revolutionary change
in the economy is a political revolution. In the Marxist
scheme, political development, depending as it does upon
economic development, cannot be a gradual evolution, a
piece-meal adaptation to changing circumstances. At some
point there must be a vast change, a change in the system
as a whole. The law of dialectical movement is not a mere
ornament of the Marxist system, but a pillar of the dogma
of revolution.

II

MARXIST THEORY OF THE DEVELOPMENT OF CAPITALISM

Some of the points in the Marxist system may become
a little clearer—some may become more obscure—if we
examine its application to the economic development of
capitalism. What we have been considering so far have
been the general laws of economic development—the
laws of the dialectical process—which apply to all the
precommunist stages. But Marx also thought that each
stage of history had its special laws and he spent many
years working out what he regarded as the more particular
law of development of capitalism, "the economic law of
motion of modern society," which he set forth in his
principal work, *Capital*. In the selection printed in this
book he summarizes the main principles of that law.

The cornerstone of Marx' economics is the labor theory
of value. This theory, which Marx shared with the fathers
of classical economics, Adam Smith and Ricardo, and with
his contemporaries, is a theory of price. How do we explain the fact that two things which are qualitatively different—for instance, a coat and a bushel of wheat—can

have the same price? What do they have in common which makes possible this equivalence? Marx' answer was "labor," meaning both the labor directly expended in producing the commodity and the labor which went into producing the tools and machinery which were used in producing it. Roughly, the more hours of labor expended on producing a thing, the greater its value. This proposition, however, he qualified by the reasonable proviso that labor not be foolishly wasted in production, but be used in accord with the existing standard of efficiency in production—it should be "the socially necessary" quantity of labor for producing such a commodity. In this sense, his labor theory of value is that the price of a commodity will be proportional to the quantity of labor directly and indirectly used in producing it.

In an undeveloped economy this theory may be plausible. Where labor is largely of one kind, and is overwhelmingly the main factor in production, prices may tend to reflect the amount of time expended in their production. In the circumstances of a modern economy, however, the theory is hopeless as an attempt to explain prices, and in Marx' own lifetime it lost most of its adherents. Marx' struggles with the theory in the later parts of *Capital* indicate that he himself hardly found it a convenient theory to use.

It is an interesting exercise to try to determine whether the main principles of Marxian economics are logically and necessarily dependent on the labor theory of value. In developing his "law of economic motion," at any rate, Marx assumed the theory and made it the foundation for a major element in his doctrine, the theory of surplus value, or exploitation. The term "exploitation" is heavy with moral condemnation and it is easy to assume that Marx is attacking capitalists and their system for "robbery," for taking from the workers what is rightfully theirs. No doubt many who have been swayed by Marx have so understood him, but this is certainly not what he meant. For, as Marx describes the process, each person receives his due; the worker receives his value, the customer pays

only what the goods are worth—yet the uncreative capitalist is left with his profits.

Marx achieves this result by making the labor theory
of value apply in a very special way to labor itself. Under
capitalism, he says, the capacity to work is a commodity
which like any other commodity is sold in the market for
its intrinsic value. Strictly speaking, what the worker sells,
Marx insists, is not his labor itself, but his capacity to
work, his labor-power. Like other commodities, therefore,
this commodity, labor-power, will have a price proportional to the amount of labor which goes into its production; that is, to the amount of labor, direct and indirect,
which is needed to keep a worker alive and enable him
to reproduce himself—a subsistence wage. Once, however,
the worker has sold his labor-power to the capitalist, he
works not only a number of hours sufficient to cover the
price paid for his labor-power by the capitalist, but also
an additional number of hours. These hours, of course,
create value and so are reflected in the price of the goods
sold to the consumer. The value they create, however, is
a surplus over and above what the worker gets. This
surplus value the capitalist takes from the process of production in the form of profit, interest, and rent.

Two questions call for an answer. Why is the worker
unable to get more wages or to work shorter hours? And
what happens to the surplus value which this process has
brought into existence? Let us consider the last question
first, as it leads to two of the sounder insights of Marxian
economics, his theories of accumulation and of centralization.

Marx does not conceive of the capitalist as a pleasure-
seeker who dissipates his profits in riotous self-indulgence.
The familiar portrait of the fat capitalist with expensive
clothes, a gold watch-chain and a big cigar, while it has
often been used by Marxist propagandists, is fundamen-
tally untrue to the Marxist theory. The Marxist capitalist
—indeed, like the true capitalist—is much more the
disciplined, self-denying captain of industry who plows his
profits back into the business, turning each increment of

profit into a new element of capital with which more profit is in turn realized. To this central process of the capitalist system—the continual reinvestment of profit by which machinery, tools, and factories are expanded and the system made more productive—Marx attached the utmost importance. Indeed, he "saw this process of industrial change more clearly and realized its pivotal importance more fully than any economist of his time." [4]

Thus do the productive forces of capitalism grow. If, however, capitalists are disciplined and self-denying, that is not because of inherent qualities of character. They accumulate because they are compelled by competition to accumulate, or go under. Neither choice, nor vision nor creative imagination play a significant role. Equally mechanical and also dominated by the blind forces of competition is the process of centralization of capital. In the ceaseless struggle for existence in the capitalist economy, the more productive firms win out over the less productive. But productivity depends on the scale of production. "Therefore, the larger capitals beat the smaller." [5] And as the smaller capitalists are beaten and in part absorbed by the larger, the number of capitalists remaining shrinks, while the size of their economic empires grows. Marx' anticipation of the advent of Big Business, like his insight into the importance of investment, was remarkable for a thinker of his time. Neither conclusion, it may be noted, depends upon the labor theory of value. Neither, indeed, need be rejected by a defender of the capitalist system, for do they not constitute a story of continual economic progress and a rising standard of living for all?

That, however, is not the story which Marx is telling. When we turn to the next step in his analysis, the plot thickens and the drama of his tale rises in inverse ratio to its plausibility. For we must now ask, what does the law of economic motion bring to the workers? The paradox —the central contradiction—of capitalism, according to

[4] Joseph Schumpeter, *Capitalism, Socialism and Democracy* (2nd edn., New York, 1947), p. 32
[5] below, p. 76

Marx, is that instead of benefiting from the process of accumulation, the workers, by that very process, are made even poorer and more miserable. This is the law of increasing misery which holds forth under capitalism as inexorably as the laws of accumulation and centralization.

Why—to return to a question asked above—are the workers unable to win higher wages and shorter hours, as in fact they have done continually throughout the last hundred years of capitalism? What prevents them from getting from the capitalist the full amount of the value they create and from sharing in the increasing productivity of the system? Marx' answer is "the industrial reserve army" which capitalism inevitably produces and which is essential if the system is to produce surplus value for the capitalist.[6]

As the objective forces of competition compel the capitalist to accumulate or go under, so the process of accumulation in turn produces the industrial reserve army. For as capital accumulates, that part of it which is spent on labor diminishes in relation to that part which is spent on the means of production. In Marxian terminology, variable capital declines in relation to constant capital. It is thus that a given amount of labor is able to transform a larger amount of the means of production into commodities and the productivity of labor grows.[7] The other side of the coin, however, is the unemployment of those workers who have lost their jobs as variable capital declines—the simplest, although not the only, case being when machines are used to replace men. Offsetting causes Marx admits, but he maintains that in the long-run compensating factors will be overborne and that "the greater the social wealth . . . the greater is the industrial reserve army." [8] By competing for jobs, this army of unemployed keeps wages down to a subsistence level and prevents the shortening of hours. Ultimately, however, the process creates that mass of proletarian misery which, converted into revolu-

[6] below, pp. 78 ff.
[7] below, pp. 71 ff.
[8] below, p. 92

tionary wrath, is the force which will overturn the capitalist system. Capitalism thus produces its own gravediggers.

But it is not only revolutionary wrath which is at work undermining capitalism. The system of production itself has begun to falter. Economic crises break out from time to time; industry and commerce are brought to a standstill and neither profits nor goods are produced. Neither Marx nor Engels ever gave a convincing explanation of business crises or of why capitalism must decline economically. They did, however, assert that there would be ever more severe crises and cited them as examples of how productive forces were fettered by the mode of production.

If we are less than satisfied with the Marxist explanation of economic crises, no more than a superficial knowledge of economic history is needed to show how wildly out of accord with the facts the "law" of increasing misery has proved to be. But whether Marx is rationally convincing or not, the emotional force of his prophecy of the apocalypse is undeniable:

While there is thus a progressive diminution in the number of the capitalist magnates (who usurp and monopolize all the advantages of this transformative process), there occurs a corresponding increase in the mass of poverty, oppression, enslavement, degeneration, and exploitation; but at the same time there is a steady intensification of the wrath of the working class—a class which grows ever more numerous, and is disciplined, unified, and organized by the very mechanism of the capitalist method of production. Capitalist monopoly becomes a fetter upon the method of production which has flourished with it and under it. The centralization of the means of production and the socialization of labor reach a point where they prove incompatible with their capitalist husk. This bursts asunder. The knell of capitalist private property sounds. The expropriators are expropriated." [9]

III

THEORY OF SUPERSTRUCTURE

The second essential of Marxism we have taken to be the notion that the mode of production, developing accord-

[9] *Capital* (Everyman edn., London, 1930), p. 846

ing to objective laws, determines all other aspects of the society. Strictly speaking, that is to say, there is one and only one chain of causation in history, the economic; all other aspects or events are causally dependent on this chain and do not in turn act causally upon it. Sometimes indeed Marx clearly departs from this strict version of economic determinism. Yet he may not go far, because it is only a strict version which is consistent with the other elements of his system and, in particular, as we shall see, with his belief in the inevitability of violent revolution.

The most striking example of this notion of economic determinism is the theory of ideology—that is, the Marxist view of the causal relation between thought and the mode of production. Marx states this theory in general terms by holding that social existence determines consciousness, not consciousness social existence.[10] We need, however, to try to see more precisely what he means. Already in our discussion of the theory of objective development we have touched on the question. We may be ready to grant to Marx that objective development sometimes occurs in the social process and that such development may show uniformities amounting to social laws. Certainly, however, we must ask why Marx does not take the next step and suggest that men should seek a knowledge of these laws in order to be able to control such developments. That is what a modern social scientist tries to do. An economist, for instance, studies economic depressions in order to learn how they may be prevented or controlled. Does Marx not think that men can gain control over social processes?

He does indeed look forward to the day when the blind forces of history will be subject to conscious, human control. In a sense, such control will be the major consequence of the transition to a communist society. Communism will bring, he writes, "the control and conscious mastery of these powers, which, born of the action of men on one another, have till now overawed and governed men as powers completely alien to them." [11] In that society and

[10] above, p. ix
[11] *The German Ideology* (New York, 1947), p. 28

because of that control, men will finally achieve perfect freedom. Before that day, however, they remain slaves to historical necessity and their thought and thinking are rigidly determined by the mode of production. "What else," says the *Manifesto*, "does the history of ideas prove than that intellectual production changes its character in proportion as material production is changed?" And he continues, making clear the line of causation: "When people speak of ideas that revolutionize society, they do but express the fact that within the old society the elements of a new one have been created, and that the dissolution of the old ideas keeps even pace with the dissolution of the old conditions of existence." [12]

Our question—and it is one of the most important of the social sciences—is this: when some new pattern of social behavior occurs—for example, a different standard of social conduct or morality, a new mode of organizing business, a reform of the constitution of a state—where shall we find its origin? One possibility is that it occurred first in someone's mind. Perhaps it was the creative idea of a statesman or poet, a businessman or administrator; possibly it emerged from a meeting of minds in some democratic assembly; very probably, if it is an idea of major importance, it came from many minds and developed over the years. At any rate, the general formula of sequence is: first the new thought, then the new pattern of behavior. Creative thinking of this sort, however, Marx entirely rules out as an influence on history. For him the formula is precisely reversed; first comes the behavior, then the thought. Where new patterns develop in history they are first produced unintentionally, blindly, in the course of objective development. Then and only then may these new forms be "reflected" in human minds. Ideas in Marxian language are merely "ideological reflexes and echoes" of man's "material life-process." [13]

What is shaped by the mode of production is thought in the widest sense: not only ideas, but ideals and interests

[12] below, p. 30
[13] *The German Ideology*, p. 14

as well. The whole subjective world of mind is determined by the objective world of the economy. When, for instance, greed or selfishness is found in the subjective world, the cause is not something inherent in human nature, nor is it controllable by moral discipline. The root, as always, is the mode of production which, by putting some men in a position to profit by the labor and suffering of others and compelling them to do so, or themselves go under, imprints the corresponding traits on the human personality. Wrathful as Marx may be in his denunciation of capitalists and the whole class of those who own and who rule, his ultimate view is that not individuals, but "the system" is to blame. Evil, like the objective development from which it is derived, is independent of human will and can only be abolished when in the fullness of time the laws of history bring into existence the perfect human community where, as Marx says, "the free development of each is the condition for the free development of all." [14]

What of ideals? Marx does not deny that ideals may be sincerely held and acted upon. The "bourgeois" ideal of justice, which he denounces, is, he would claim, merely a reflection of the interests of the capitalist class and mode of production. The bourgeoisie, however, do not know this; indeed, they are so much the creatures of ideology that they are incapable of seeing it even when it is pointed out to them. So while they do not fool Marx, they do fool themselves, and their protestations of horror at the communist program are sincere, though worthless.

It also follows that such ideals cannot be called upon to bring about the reform of society. Marx' socialist contemporaries for the most part appealed to the conscience, ideals or better instincts of the owning class for aid and leadership in carrying on their movement. With scorn Marx rejected these appeals to moral feelings. And necessarily so in terms of his conception of history: the mode of production determines ideals; they can hardly be used to change it.

Why not? Why indeed must thought be so narrowly limited by economic conditions? Marx certainly allows that

[14] below, p. 32

men can make inventions which raise the efficiency of production. The advance of technology and science generally, while limited to innovations which are relevant to the needs of the time, nevertheless, has a real part in bringing about historical development. Why then can there not be an advance in "social technology" or "social engineering?" Why in other branches than the technical are men barred by ideology from thinking creatively? But if this question goes without an answer from Marx, even more important is his failure ever to suggest a plausible foundation for his theory of ideology in general. Anyone will grant that economic conditions "affect" the thinking of the time—sometimes more, sometimes less—and one of the most interesting tasks of intellectual history is to try to examine the relationship between thought and economics in particular periods. Marx, however, was not interested in framing interesting tasks for historians, but in stating a fundamental dogma of his revolutionary faith.

Upon this dogma depends the rest of his theory of the social superstructure, of which we may consider his theory of classes and his theory of the state. In the Marxian scheme a class is a set of persons all of whom stand in the same objective relationship to the mode of production. The main division, is, of course, between those who own the means of production and those who do not. Within these classes, however, there may be further distinctions, depending upon the stage of economic development. For instance, in the early period of capitalism, there will be a large class of small owners—craftsmen, shopkeepers, peasants—who because of their economic position will have interests and ideas different from both the large capitalists and the propertyless workers. Analyzing society in these terms, Marx made many forays into the history of his times with results which were often at the same time brilliant and wrong-headed. One is the *Eighteenth Brumaire of Louis Bonaparte* from which selections are reprinted below and which is probably the best of his analyses.

Like the class structure, the state—meaning by this both political institutions and the system of law—also is determined by the mode of production. "Political power," says the *Manifesto,* "is merely the organized power of one class for oppressing another." [15] Each of the three modes of production based on private property has had its corresponding state-form in which, according to Engels, "the most powerful, economically dominant class . . . by virtue thereof becomes also the dominant class politically." [16] Like the slave-owners' state and the feudal state, the modern representative state is a "means of holding down and exploiting the oppressed class." Being such an instrument, however, the state has not always existed. In the stage of primitive communism, since there was no owning class, there was no state. Only after private property had been brought into existence by economic development did the state arise.

At first glance, the theory would seem to be that it is the force of the state which keeps the owning class in control of the means of production. And indeed, this would be plausible. For in actual fact, if individuals and other private units of ownership are secure in their control of the means of production, one good reason is that the law backed by public force guarantees their private property. But Marx cannot and does not say this, for to say so would be equivalent to saying that economic power is founded upon political power, quite the reverse of economic determinism. The law which establishes private property must, therefore, in some sense be a reflection of the objective facts of the mode of production. Far from being founded on *a priori* principles of justice, it is, like other elements in the ideology of the ruling class—as the *Manifesto* says, addressing the bourgeoisie—simply "the will of your class made into a law for all, a will whose essential character and direction are determined by the economic conditions of existence of your class." [17] In the causal series first comes the objective necessity of individual control arising from the stage of development

[15] below, p. 32
[16] Engels, *The Origin of the Family, Private Property and the State.* In E. Burns (ed.), *Handbook of Marxism* (New York, 1935), p. 330.
[17] below, p. 27

of the productive forces. Following this necessity is the law establishing that particular system of private property appropriate to the mode of production.

What is this "objective necessity" behind the various systems of property? Why, for instance, was the system of primitive communism unable to continue as the productive forces developed? Why could not its methods of communal control have been adapted to the higher stages of economic development? Neither Marx nor Engels, nor for that matter their disciples, have given a satisfactory answer. Here in the face of one of the most important problems of the materialist conception—its version, so to speak, of how evil came into the world—we are faced with an insuperable difficulty. Nor is this a problem merely of origins. If it is to be argued, as Marx does, that during the three noncommunist stages of history, private property is the only possible form of legal system, it must be shown that an objective necessity continues to require it.

While the Marxist system maintains that private property is inevitable during the intermediate stages of history, it nevertheless does allow some role for physical force and political power. The social system is not frictionless; as economic forces come into conflict, class behavior reflects that fact and those class struggles ensue of which Marx says the previous history of man has been largely composed. To prevent such struggles from disrupting the economy, the state is used by the ruling class to maintain the mode of production to which its class interest is irrevocably attached. To a certain extent, therefore, a noneconomic factor—i.e. the physical force which the state wields—has a causal role. That role, however, is narrowly circumscribed. For when the point of transition is reached, the force in the hands of the old ruling class cannot suffice to maintain the old conditions. The class representing the new mode of production will amass the power necessary to overthrow the old regime. It must do this by violence; and sooner or later it is bound to win.

Why must the revolution be violent? All elements in the Marxist system conspire to that conclusion, but in the

Marxist theory of ideology lies the immediate answer. For the sake of an example, consider the situation of the capitalist class in the declining days of their system. Their minds, their ideas and interests, are formed by their relationship to the mode of production. They cannot wish to alter it; indeed, they are incapable of thinking their way through to a solution. As difficulties pile up, they will resort to all sorts of superficial stratagems. Marx describes some of these in Part III of the *Manifesto* under the heading of the different varieties of "socialism" to which he was opposed. All these proposals, according to Marx, are mere palliatives; they come down to "administrative reforms" based on the continued existence of capitalism and the acceptance of it by the proletariat. They demonstrate the inability of the bourgeoisie to think beyond their system. All the while, however, the proletariat is gaining in strength, in unity and organization, while the declining capitalist system is losing its economic power. This superior proletarian force will, and only this force can, overthrow the system.

In terms of Marxist doctrine, violent revolution is the only way out. To see this, we need only reason back from a different conclusion. Suppose we assert that the transition to socialism can be made peacefully—that is, with the consent of the capitalists. This, of course, implies that the capitalists have thought beyond the forms of the capitalist system. But once we grant that possibility, it follows that thought and will in the past may not have been wholly or always determined by the mode of production. And this in turn implies that economic development itself may have been brought about by creative thought as well as by objective development. Our grand materialist conception of history is reduced to a proposition of "more or less." "To a great extent" and "sometimes" or "often," the economy affects the rest of society; sometimes thought takes the lead in historical development, sometimes the unintended forces of the economy. All this may sound like cautious, good sense; it is not the Marxian prophecy.

One final doctrine of that prophecy remains to be considered: the transition to communism.

Once the capitalist state has been overthrown by the proletarian revolution, what then? In essence, the historical process no longer has need of the state. The productive powers have developed to the point at which not only capitalism, but any form of individual control is unnecessary and, indeed, impossible. It follows that private property and the means of protecting it, the state, are no longer necessary. Marx, however, allows for an intermediate period when ideas and interests inherited from the old economy still have some influence. This period he calls socialism and while the economy is now communally controlled, individuals—all of whom now are workers—receive their means of existence according to "bourgeois right," i.e. in accord with their contribution to production.

During this time, also, a form of state remains. Marx used the term "dictatorship of the proletariat" to describe it.[18] This state was not dictatorship in the sense of rule by one man or a few; on the contrary, as he conceived it, this state would be a democracy, in which the majority—the proletariat—exercised dictatorship only over the minority—the remnants of the bourgeoisie.

In time, however, as "cultural lag" was overcome, even this form of state would no longer be needed. Then in Engels' expressive phrase, it would "wither away." [19] Force would vanish from the relations of men. The administration of things would take the place of the administration of men. Likewise the mode of distribution would change and now instead of each person being paid in accord with what he produced, the principle of distribution would be "from each according to his ability, to each according to his needs." [20] A society which once again could be called communist would have arrived, and as force had vanished, so also would selfishness. After having

[18] Marx and Engels, *Selected Correspondence,* 1846-95 (New York, 1942), p. 57. Marx, *The Civil War in France* (New York, 1933), *passim,* and its preface by Engels.
[19] *Anti-Duehring* in E. Burns (ed.), *A Handbook of Marxism* (New York, 1935), p. 296
[20] *Critique of the Gotha Programme* in *Selected Works* (London, 1942), Vol. II, p. 566

been so long alienated from his true self, man would at last through the grace of the iron laws of history enter into his earthly paradise, where all live together in perfect freedom and community.

This final vision of Marx is ancient and in no sense ignoble. His is, however, a vision—a dangerous vision. To teach that evil arises only from economic institutions is false. Men may be corrupted by power as well as by property and in any society pride will find ways of distorting human nature. To found a movement or a state upon a doctrine which does not recognize these possibilities is an invitation to tyranny.

PRINCIPAL DATES IN THE LIFE
OF KARL MARX

1818 Born in Trier, Germany, son of a lawyer.

1835-41 Studied at universities of Bonn and Berlin; received doctorate of philosophy.

1842-43 Editor, *Rheinische Zeitung,* liberal-democratic journal, suppressed by Prussian authorities.

1843 Married Jenny von Westphalen, daughter of Prussian aristocrat. Moved to Paris where he made the acquaintance of Friedrich Engels (1820-1895), son of a wealthy textile manufacturer.

1847 *The Poverty of Philosophy.*

1848 *The Communist Manifesto,* on which Engels collaborated, published for the Communist League in London.

1849 Expelled from Prussia after acquittal in trial for high treason; settled in London.

1852 *The 18th Brumaire of Louis Bonaparte.*

1859 *The Critique of Political Economy.*

1864 International Workingmen's Association founded.

1867 Volume I, *Capital.*

1875 *Critique of the Gotha Program.*

1883 Died in London.

POSTHUMOUS PUBLICATIONS

1885 Volume II, *Capital* (completed by Engels).

1894 Volume III, *Capital* (completed by Engels).

MANIFESTO OF THE COMMUNIST PARTY

PREFACE TO THE ENGLISH EDITION OF 1888

By Friedrich Engels

THE *Manifesto* was published as the platform of the Communist League, a workingmen's association, first exclusively German, later on international, and, under the political conditions of the Continent before 1848, unavoidably a secret society. At a Congress of the League, held in London in November, 1847, Marx and Engels were commissioned to prepare for publication a complete theoretical and practical party program. Drawn up in German, in January, 1848, the manuscript was sent to the printer in London a few weeks before the French revolution of February 24th.[1] A French translation was brought out in Paris, shortly before the insurrection of June, 1848. The first English translation, by Miss Helen Macfarlane, appeared in George Julian Harney's *Red Republican*, London, 1850. A Danish and a Polish edition had also been published.

The defeat of the Parisian insurrection of June, 1848— the first great battle between proletariat and bourgeoisie— drove again into the background, for a time, the social and political aspirations of the European working class. Thenceforth, the struggle for supremacy was again, as it had been before the revolution of February, solely between different sections of the propertied class; the work-

[1] As a result of the revolution in Paris, February 22-24, 1848, Louis Philippe was deposed and a republic proclaimed. Later the republic was overthrown by Louis Bonaparte, the nephew of Napoleon I. See below, pp. 47 ff.

1

ing class was reduced to a fight for political elbow-room, and to the position of extreme wing of the middle-class Radicals. Wherever independent proletarian movements continued to show signs of life, they were ruthlessly hunted down. Thus the Prussian police hunted out the Central Board of the Communist League, then located in Cologne. The members were arrested, and, after eighteen months' imprisonment, they were tried in October, 1852. This celebrated "Cologne Communist Trial" lasted from October 4th till November 12th; seven of the prisoners were sentenced to terms of imprisonment in a fortress, varying from three to six years. Immediately after the sentence, the League was formally dissolved by the remaining members. As to the *Manifesto*, it seemed thenceforth to be doomed to oblivion.

When the European working class had recovered sufficient strength for another attack on the ruling classes, the International Workingmen's Association sprang up.[2] But this association, formed with the express aim of welding into one body the whole militant proletariat of Europe and America, could not at once proclaim the principles laid down in the *Manifesto*. The International was bound to have a program broad enough to be acceptable to the English trades unions, to the followers of Proudhon[3] in France, Belgium, Italy, and Spain, and to the Lassalleans[4] in Germany. Marx, who drew up this program to the satisfaction of all parties, entirely trusted to the intellectual development of the working class, which was sure to result

[2] Founded in 1864, Marx taking a leading part
[3] Pierre Joseph Proudhon (1809-1865), French socialist, author of *The Philosophy of Poverty* (1846), which Marx attacked in his early work, *The Poverty of Philosophy* (1847)
[4] Ferdinand Lassalle (1825-1864), German socialist leader, founded in 1863 the General German Workingmen's Association, one of the sources of the Social Democratic party
[Note by Engels] Lassalle always acknowledged himself to us personally to be a disciple of Marx and, as such, stood on the ground of the *Manifesto*. But in his public agitation, 1862-64, he did not go beyond demanding co-operative workshops supported by state credit.

from combined action and mutual discussion. The very events and vicissitudes of the struggle against capital, the defeats even more than the victories, could not help bringing home to men's minds the insufficiency of their various favorite nostrums, and preparing the way for a more complete insight into the true conditions of working-class emancipation. And Marx was right. The International, on its breaking up in 1874, left the workers quite different men from what it had found them in 1864. Proudhonism in France, Lassalleanism in Germany were dying out, and even the conservative English trades unions, though most of them had long since severed their connection with the International, were gradually advancing towards that point at which, last year at Swansea, their president could say in their name "continental Socialism has lost its terrors for us." In fact, the principles of the *Manifesto* had made considerable headway among the workingmen of all countries.

The *Manifesto* itself thus came to the front again. Since 1850 the German text had been reprinted several times in Switzerland, England, and America. In 1872, it was translated into English in New York, where the translation was published in *Woodhull and Claflin's Weekly*. From this English version, a French one was made in *Le Socialiste* of New York. Since then at least two more English translations, more or less mutilated, have been brought out in America, and one of them has been reprinted in England. The first Russian translation, made by Bakunin,[5] was published at Herzen's[6] *Kolokol* office in Geneva, about 1863; a second one, by the heroic Vera Zasulich, also in Geneva, in 1882.[7] A new Danish edition is to be found in *Socialde-*

[5] **Mikhail Bakunin** (1814-1876), Russian anarchist, who although an advocate of proletarian revolution, broke with Marx over the latter's view that a form of the state—the dictatorship of the proletariat—would be maintained after the revolution and during the transition to communism

[6] **Alexander Herzen** (1812-1870), Russian author and socialist, published in exile a periodical *Kolokol* (The Bell) which had considerable influence in Russia and Europe generally

[7] The Russian version of 1882 was not by **Vera Zasulich,** but by **Georgei Plekhanov** (1857-1918), the founder of Russian Marxism

mokratisk Bibliothek, Copenhagen. 1885; a fresh French translation in *Le Socialiste,* Paris, 1886. From this latter, a Spanish version was prepared and published in Madrid, in 1886. Not counting the German reprints there had been at least twelve editions. An Armenian translation, which was to be published in Constantinople some months ago, did not see the light, I am told, because the publisher was afraid of bringing out a book with the name of Marx on it, while the translator declined to call it his own production. Of further translations into other languages I have heard, but have not seen. Thus the history of the *Manifesto* reflects, to a great extent, the history of the modern working class movement; at present it is undoubtedly the most widespread, the most international production of all Socialist literature, the common platform acknowledged by millions of workingmen from Siberia to California.

Yet, when it was written, we could not have called it a *Socialist* manifesto. By Socialists, in 1847, were understood, on the one hand, the adherents of the various Utopian systems: Owenites in England, Fourierists in France,[8] both of them already reduced to the position of mere sects, and gradually dying out; on the other hand, the most multifarious social quacks, who, by all manners of tinkering, professed to redress, without any danger to capital and profit, all sorts of social grievances, in both cases men outside the working class movement, and looking rather to the "educated" classes for support. Whatever portion of the working class had become convinced of the insufficiency of mere political revolutions, and had proclaimed the necessity of a total social change, called itself Communist. It was a crude, rough-hewn, purely instinctive sort of Communism; still, it touched the cardinal point and was powerful enough amongst the working class to pro-

[8] Robert Owen (1771-1858), forerunner of socialism and the co-operative movement in Britain, advocated the establishment of small communist colonies under paternalistic rule. The communities proposed by François Charles Fourier (1772-1837), were based on the *phalanstère,* or common building, in which all families lived, and permitted complete freedom to all members.

duce the Utopian Communism of Cabet[9] in France, and of Weitling[10] in Germany. Thus, in 1847, Socialism was a middle-class movement, communism a working-class movement. Socialism was, on the continent at least, "respectable"; communism was the very opposite. And as our notion, from the very beginning, was that "the emancipation of the working class must be the act of the working class itself," there could be no doubt as to which of the two names we must take. Moreover, we have, ever since, been far from repudiating it.

The *Manifesto* being our joint production, I consider myself bound to state that the fundamental proposition which forms its nucleus, belongs to Marx. That proposition is: That in every historical epoch, the prevailing mode of economic production and exchange, and the social organization necessarily following from it, form the basis upon which is built up, and from which alone can be explained, the political and intellectual history of that epoch; that consequently the whole history of mankind (since the dissolution of primitive tribal society, holding land in common ownership) has been a history of class struggles, contests between exploiting and exploited, ruling and oppressed classes; that the history of these class struggles form a series of evolutions in which, nowadays, a stage has been reached where the exploited and oppressed class— the proletariat—cannot attain its emancipation from the sway of the exploiting and ruling class—the bourgeoisie— without at the same time, and once and for all, emancipat-

---

[9] Etienne Cabet (1788-1856), French socialist and author of *Voyage en Icarie* in which he depicted life in a communist society. His doctrine, like that of Owen and Fourier, was dubbed "utopian" by Engels because it was not founded upon the "scientific" theory of history developed by Marx.

[10] Wilhelm Weitling (1808-1871), a German tailor and leader of the League of the Just, an international society of proletarian revolutionaries which preceded the Communist League. An early friend of Marx, who later attacked him bitterly, he emigrated to the United States where he continued his socialist agitation.

ing society at large from all exploitation, oppression, class distinctions and class struggles.

This proposition, which, in my opinion, is destined to do for history what Darwin's theory has done for biology, we, both of us, had been gradually approaching for some years before 1845. How far I had independently progressed towards it, is best shown by my *Condition of the Working Class in England*. But when I again met Marx at Brussels, in spring, 1845, he had it already worked out, and put it before me, in terms almost as clear as those in which I have stated it here.

From our joint preface to the German edition of 1872, I quote:

However much the state of things may have altered during the last 25 years, the general principles laid down in this *Manifesto* are, on the whole, as correct today as ever. Here and there some detail might be improved. The practical application of the principles will depend, as the *Manifesto* itself states, everywhere and at all times, on the historical conditions for the time being existing, and, for that reason, no special stress is laid on the revolutionary measures proposed at the end of Section II. That passage would, in many respects, be very differently worded today. In view of the gigantic strides of modern industry since 1848, and of the accompanying improved and extended organization of the working class, in view of the practical experience gained, first in the February revolution, and then, still more, in the Paris Commune,[11] where the proletariat for the first time held political power for two whole months, this program has in some details become antiquated. One thing especially was proved by the Commune, *viz.*, that "the working class cannot simply lay hold of the ready-made state machinery, and wield it for its own purposes." (See *The Civil War in France; Address by the General Council of the International Workingmen's Association*, 1871, where this point is further developed.) Further, it is self-evident, that the criticism of Socialist literature is deficient in relation to the present time, because it comes down only to 1847; also, that the remarks on the relation of the Communists to the various opposition parties (Section IV), although in principle still correct, yet in practice are antiquated, because the political situation has been entirely changed, and the progress

[11] The insurrectionary government which took possession of Paris at the end of the Franco-Prussian War in 1871

of history has swept from off the earth the greater portion of the political parties there enumerated.

But then, the *Manifesto* has become a historical document which we have no longer any right to alter.

The present translation is by Mr. Samuel Moore, the translator of the greater portion of Marx's *Capital*. We have revised it in common, and I have added a few notes explanatory of historical allusions.

London, January 30th, 1888.

MANIFESTO OF THE COMMUNIST PARTY

By KARL MARX and FRIEDRICH ENGELS

A SPECTER is haunting Europe—the specter of communism. All the powers of old Europe have entered into a holy alliance to exorcise this specter: Pope and Czar, Metternich and Guizot,[1] French Radicals[2] and German police spies.

Where is the party in opposition that has not been decried as communistic by its opponents in power? Where the Opposition that has not hurled back the branding reproach of communism, against the more advanced opposition parties, as well as against its reactionary adversaries?

Two things result from this fact:

I. Communism is already acknowledged by all European powers to be itself a power.

II. It is high time that Communists should openly, in the face of the whole world, publish their views, their aims, their tendencies, and meet this nursery tale of the specter of communism with a manifesto of the party itself.

To this end, Communists of various nationalities have assembled in London, and sketched the following manifesto, to be published in the English, French, German, Italian, Flemish, and Danish languages.

[1] Prince von Metternich (1773-1859), chancellor of the Austrian empire. François Pierre Guizot (1787-1874), French historian and statesman, prime minister at the time of the revolution of 1848
[2] French Radicals, radical republicans

I

BOURGEOIS AND PROLETARIANS[1]

The history of all hitherto existing society[2] is the history of class struggles.

Freeman and slave, patrician and plebeian, lord and serf, guildmaster[3] and journeyman, in a word, oppressor and oppressed, stood in constant opposition to one another, carried on an uninterrupted, now hidden, now open fight, a fight that each time ended, either in a revolutionary reconstitution of society at large, or in the common ruin of the contending classes.

In the earlier epochs of history, we find almost every-

---

[1] In French bourgeois means a town-dweller. "Proletarian" comes from the Latin, proletarius, which meant a person whose sole wealth was his offspring (proles).

[Note by Engels] By "bourgeoisie" is meant the class of modern capitalists, owners of the means of social production and employers of wage-labor; by "proletariat," the class of modern wage-laborers who, having no means of production of their own, are reduced to selling their labor power in order to live.

[2] [Note by Engels] That is, all written history. In 1837, the prehistory of society, the social organization existing previous to recorded history, was all but unknown. Since then Haxthausen [August von, 1792-1866] discovered common ownership of land in Russia, Maurer [Georg Ludwig von] proved it to be the social foundation from which all Teutonic races started in history, and, by and by, village communities were found to be, or to have been, the primitive form of society everywhere from India to Ireland. The inner organization of this primitive communistic society was laid bare, in its typical form, by Morgan's [Lewis H., 1818-1881] crowning discovery of the true nature of the gens and its relation to the tribe. With the dissolution of these primeval communities, society begins to be differentiated into separate and finally antagonistic classes. I have attempted to retrace this process of dissolution in The Origin of the Family, Private Property and the State.

[3] [Note by Engels] Guild-master, that is a full member of a guild, a master within, not a head of a guild

where a complicated arrangement of society into various orders, a manifold gradation of social rank. In ancient Rome we have patricians, knights, plebeians, slaves; in the Middle Ages, feudal lords, vassals, guild-masters, journeymen, apprentices, serfs; in almost all of these classes, again, subordinate gradations.

The modern bourgeois society that has sprouted from the ruins of feudal society, has not done away with class antagonisms. It has but established new classes, new conditions of oppression, new forms of struggle in place of the old ones.

Our epoch, the epoch of the bourgeoisie, possesses, however, this distinctive feature: It has simplified the class antagonisms. Society as a whole is more and more splitting up into two great hostile camps, into two great classes directly facing each other—bourgeoisie and proletariat.

From the serfs of the Middle Ages sprang the chartered burghers of the earliest towns. From these burgesses the first elements of the bourgeoisie were developed.

The discovery of America, the rounding of the Cape, opened up fresh ground for the rising bourgeoisie. The East-Indian and Chinese markets, the colonization of America, trade with the colonies, the increase in the means of exchange and in commodities generally, gave to commerce, to navigation, to industry, an impulse never before known, and thereby, to the revolutionary element in the tottering feudal society, a rapid development.

The feudal system of industry, in which industrial production was monopolized by closed guilds, now no longer sufficed for the growing wants of the new markets. The manufacturing system took its place. The guild-masters were pushed aside by the manufacturing middle class; division of labor between the different corporate guilds vanished in the face of division of labor in each single workshop.

Meantime the markets kept ever growing, the demand ever rising. Even manufacture[4] no longer sufficed. There-

[4] By **manufacture** Marx meant the system of production which succeeded the guild system but which still relied mainly upon direct human labor for power. He distinguished it from modern

upon, steam and machinery revolutionized industrial production. The place of manufacture was taken by the giant, modern industry, the place of the industrial middle class, by industrial millionaires—the leaders of whole industrial armies, the modern bourgeois.

Modern industry has established the world market, for which the discovery of America paved the way. This market has given an immense development to commerce, to navigation, to communication by land. This development has, in its turn, reacted on the extension of industry; and in proportion as industry, commerce, navigation, railways extended, in the same proportion the bourgeoisie developed, increased its capital, and pushed into the background every class handed down from the Middle Ages.

We see, therefore, how the modern bourgeoisie is itself the product of a long course of development, of a series of revolutions in the modes of production and of exchange.

Each step in the development of the bourgeoisie was accompanied by a corresponding political advance of that class. An oppressed class under the sway of the feudal nobility, it became an armed and self-governing association in the medieval commune;[5] here independent urban republic (as in Italy and Germany), there taxable "third estate" of the monarchy (as in France); afterwards, in the period of manufacture proper, serving either the semi-feudal or the absolute monarchy as a counterpoise against the nobility, and, in fact, cornerstone of the great monarchies in general—the bourgeoisie has at last, since the establishment of modern industry and of the world market, conquered for itself, in the modern representative state, exclusive political sway. The executive of the modern state

industry which arose when machinery driven by water and steam was introduced.

[5] [Note by Engels] "Commune" was the name taken in France by the nascent towns even before they had conquered from their feudal lords and masters local self-government and political rights as the "Third Estate." Generally speaking, for the economic development of the bourgeoisie, England is here taken as the typical country, for its political development, France.

is but a committee for managing the common affairs of the whole bourgeoisie.

The bourgeoisie has played a most revolutionary role in history.

The bourgeoisie, wherever it has got the upper hand, has put an end to all feudal, patriarchal, idyllic relations. It has pitilessly torn asunder the motley feudal ties that bound man to his "natural superiors," and has left no other bond between man and man than naked self-interest, than callous "cash payment." It has drowned the most heavenly ecstasies of religious fervor, of chivalrous enthusiasm, of philistine sentimentalism, in the icy water of egotistical calculation. It has resolved personal worth into exchange value, and in place of the numberless indefeasible chartered freedoms, has set up that single, unconscionable freedom—Free Trade. In one word, for exploitation, veiled by religious and political illusions, it has substituted naked, shameless, direct, brutal exploitation.

The bourgeoisie has stripped of its halo every occupation hitherto honored and looked up to with reverent awe. It has converted the physician, the lawyer, the priest, the poet, the man of science, into its paid wage-laborers.

The bourgeoisie has torn away from the family its sentimental veil, and has reduced the family relation to a mere money relation.

The bourgeoisie has disclosed how it came to pass that the brutal display of vigor in the Middle Ages, which reactionaries so much admire, found its fitting complement in the most slothful indolence. It has been the first to show what man's activity can bring about. It has accomplished wonders far surpassing Egyptian pyramids, Roman aqueducts, and Gothic cathedrals; it has conducted expeditions that put in the shade all former migrations of nations and crusades.

The bourgoisie cannot exist without constantly revolutionizing the instruments of production, and thereby the relations of production, and with them the whole relations of society. Conservation of the old modes of production in unaltered form, was, on the contrary, the first condition of existence for all earlier industrial classes. Constant revolutionizing of production, uninterrupted disturbance of all social conditions, everlasting uncertainty and agitation distinguish the bourgeois epoch from all earlier ones. All fixed, fast-frozen relations, with their train of ancient and venerable prejudices and opinions, are swept away, all new-formed ones become antiquated before they can ossify. All that is solid melts into air, all that is holy is profaned, and man is at last compelled to face with sober senses his real conditions of life and his relations with his kind.

The need of a constantly expanding market for its products chases the bourgeoisie over the whole surface of the globe. It must nestle everywhere, settle everywhere, establish connections everywhere.

The bourgeoisie has through its exploitation of the world market given a cosmopolitan character to production and consumption in every country. To the great chagrin of reactionaries, it has drawn from under the feet of industry the national ground on which it stood. All old-established national industries have been destroyed or are daily being destroyed. They are dislodged by new industries, whose introduction becomes a life and death question for all civilized nations, by industries that no longer work up indigenous raw material, but raw material drawn from the remotest zones; industries whose products are consumed, not only at home, but in every quarter of the globe. In place of the old wants, satisfied by the production of the country, we find new wants, requiring for their satisfaction the products of distant lands and climes. In place of the old local and national seclusion and self-sufficiency, we have intercourse in every direction, universal interdependence of nations. And as in material, so also in intellectual production. The intellectual creations of individual nations become common property. National one-sidedness and narrow-mindedness become more and more impossible, and from the numerous national and local literatures there arises a world literature.

The bourgeoisie, by the rapid improvement of all instruments of production, by the immensely facilitated means of communication, draws all nations, even the most barbarian, into civilization. The cheap prices of its commodities are the heavy artillery with which it batters down all Chinese walls, with which it forces the barbarians' intensely obstinate hatred of foreigners to capitulate. It compels all nations, on pain of extinction, to adopt the bourgeois mode of production; it compels them to introduce what it calls civilization into their midst, *i.e.*, to become bourgeois themselves. In a word, it creates a world after its own image.

The bourgeoisie has subjected the country to the rule of the towns. It has created enormous cities, has greatly increased the urban population as compared with the rural, and has thus rescued a considerable part of the population from the idiocy of rural life. Just as it has made the country dependent on the towns, so it has made barbarian and semibarbarian countries dependent on the civilized ones, nations of peasants on nations of bourgeois, the East on the West.

More and more the bourgeoisie keeps doing away with the scattered state of the population, of the means of production, and of property. It has agglomerated population, centralized means of production, and has concentrated property in a few hands. The necessary consequence of this was political centralization. Independent, or but loosely connected provinces, with separate interests, laws, governments and systems of taxation, became lumped together into one nation, with one government, one code of laws, one national class interest, one frontier and one customs tariff.

The bourgeoisie, during its rule of scarce one hundred years, has created more massive and more colossal productive forces than have all preceding generations together. Subjection of nature's forces to man, machinery, application of chemistry to industry and agriculture, steam-navigation, railways, electric telegraphs, clearing of whole continents for cultivation, canalization of rivers, whole populations conjured out of the ground—what earlier century had even a presentiment that such productive forces slumbered in the lap of social labor?

We see then that the means of production and of exchange, which served as the foundation for the growth of the bourgeoisie, were generated in feudal society. At a certain stage in the development of these means of production and of exchange, the conditions under which feudal society produced and exchanged, the feudal organization of agriculture and manufacturing industry, in a word, the feudal relations of property became no longer compatible with the already developed productive forces; they became so many fetters. They had to be burst asunder; they were burst asunder.

Into their place stepped free competition, accompanied by a social and political constitution adapted to it, and by the economic and political sway of the bourgeois class.

A similar movement is going on before our own eyes. Modern bourgeois society with its relations of production, of exchange and of property, a society that has conjured up such gigantic means of production and of exchange, is like the sorcerer who is no longer able to control the powers of the nether world whom he has called up by his spells. For many a decade past the history of industry and commerce is but the history of the revolt of modern productive forces against modern conditions of production, against the property relations that are the conditions for the existence of the bourgeoisie and of its rule. It is enough to mention the commercial crises that by their periodical return put the existence of the entire bourgeois society on trial, each time more threateningly. In these crises a great part not only of the existing products, but also of the previously created productive forces, are periodically destroyed. In these crises there breaks out an epidemic that, in all earlier epochs, would have seemed an absurdity— the epidemic of overproduction. Society suddenly finds itself put back into a state of momentary barbarism; it appears as if a famine, a universal war of devastation had cut off the supply of every means of subsistence; industry and commerce seem to be destroyed. And why? Because there is too much civilization, too much means of subsistence, too much industry, too much commerce. The productive forces at the disposal of society no longer tend to further the development of the conditions of bourgeois property; on the contrary, they have become too powerful for these conditions, by which they are fettered, and no sooner do they overcome these fetters than they bring disorder into the whole of bourgeois society, endanger the existence of bourgeois property. The conditions of bourgeois society are too narrow to comprise the wealth created by them. And how does the bourgeoisie get over these crises? On the one hand by enforced destruction of a mass of productive forces; on the other, by the conquest of new markets, and by the more thorough exploitation of the old ones. That is to say, by paving the way for more extensive and more destructive crises, and by diminishing the means whereby crises are prevented.

The weapons with which the bourgeoisie felled feudalism to the ground are now turned against the bourgeoisie itself.

But not only has the bourgeoisie forged the weapons that bring death to itself; it has also called into existence the men who are to wield those weapons—the modern working class—the proletarians.

In proportion as the bourgeoisie, *i.e.*, capital, is developed, in the same proportion is the proletariat, the modern working class, developed—a class of laborers, who live only so long as they find work, and who find work only so long as their labor increases capital. These laborers, who must sell themselves piecemeal, are a commodity, like every other article of commerce, and are consequently exposed to all the vicissitudes of competition, to all the fluctuations of the market.

Owing to the extensive use of machinery and to division of labor, the work of the proletarians has lost all individual character, and, consequently, all charm for the workman. He becomes an appendage of the machine, and it is only the most simple, most monotonous, and most easily acquired knack, that is required of him. Hence, the cost of production of a workman is restricted, almost entirely, to the means of subsistence that he requires for his maintenance, and for the propagation of his race. But the price of a commodity, and therefore also of labor, is equal to its cost of production. In proportion, therefore, as the repulsiveness of the work increases, the wage decreases. Nay more, in proportion as the use of machinery and division of labor increases, in the same proportion the burden of toil also increases, whether by prolongation of the working hours, by increase of the work exacted in a given time, or by increased speed of the machinery, etc.

Modern industry has converted the little workshop of the patriarchal master into the great factory of the industrial capitalist. Masses of laborers, crowded into the factory, are organized like soldiers. As privates of the industrial army they are placed under the command of a perfect hierarchy of officers and sergeants. Not only are they slaves of the bourgeois class, and of the bourgeois state; they are daily and hourly enslaved by the machine, by the overlooker, and, above all, by the individual bourgeois manufacturer himself. The more openly this despotism proclaims gain to be its end and aim, the more petty, the more hateful and the more embittering it is.

The less the skill and exertion of strength implied in manual labor, in other words, the more modern industry develops, the more is the labor of men superseded by that of women. Differences of age and sex have no longer any distinctive social validity for the working class. All are instruments of labor, more or less expensive to use, according to their age and sex.

No sooner has the laborer received his wages in cash, for the moment escaping exploitation by the manufacturer, than he is set upon by the other portions of the bourgeoisie, the landlord, the shopkeeper, the pawnbroker, etc.

The lower strata of the middle class—the small tradespeople, shopkeepers, and retired tradesmen[6] generally, the handicraftsmen and peasants—all these sink gradually into the proletariat, partly because their diminutive capital does not suffice for the scale on which modern industry is carried on, and is swamped in the competition with the large capitalists, partly because their specialized skill is rendered

[6] The word in the German original, *Rentier*, in this passage refers to a small property-owner living on unearned income from invested capital

worthless by new methods of production. Thus the proletariat is recruited from all classes of the population.

The proletariat goes through various stages of development. With its birth begins its struggle with the bourgeoisie. At first the contest is carried on by individual laborers, then by the work people of a factory, then by the operatives of one trade, in one locality, against the individual bourgeois who directly exploits them. They direct their attacks not against the bourgeois conditions of production, but against the instruments of production themselves; they destroy imported wares that compete with their labor, they smash machinery to pieces, they set factories ablaze, they seek to restore by force the vanished status of the workman of the Middle Ages.

At this stage the laborers still form an incoherent mass scattered over the whole country, and broken up by their mutual competition. If anywhere they unite to form more compact bodies, this is not yet the consequence of their own active union, but of the union of the bourgeoisie, which class, in order to attain its own political ends, is compelled to set the whole proletariat in motion, and is moreover still able to do so for a time. At this stage, therefore, the proletarians do not fight their enemies, but the enemies of their enemies, the remnants of absolute monarchy, the landowners, the nonindustrial bourgeois, the petty bourgeoisie. Thus the whole historical movement is concentrated in the hands of the bourgeoisie; every victory so obtained is a victory for the bourgeoisie.

But with the development of industry the proletariat not only increases in number; it becomes concentrated in greater masses, its strength grows, and it feels that strength more. The various interests and conditions of life within the ranks of the proletariat are more and more equalized, in proportion as machinery obliterates all distinctions of labor and nearly everywhere reduces wages to the same low level. The growing competition among the bourgeois, and the resulting commercial crises, make the wages of the workers ever more fluctuating. The unceasing improvement of machinery, ever more rapidly developing, makes their livelihood more and more precarious; the collisions between individual workmen and individual bourgeois take more and more the character of collisions between two classes. Thereupon the workers begin to form combinations (trade unions) against the bourgeoisie; they club together in order to keep up the rate of wages; they found permanent associations in order to make provision beforehand for these occasional revolts. Here and there the contest breaks out into riots.

Now and then the workers are victorious, but only for a time. The real fruit of their battles lies, not in the immediate results, but in the ever expanding union of the workers. This union is furthered by the improved means of communication which are created by modern industry, and which place the workers of different localities in contact with one another. It was just this contact that was needed to centralize the numerous local struggles, all of the same character, into one national struggle between classes. But every class struggle is a political struggle. And that union, to attain which the burghers of the Middle Ages, with their miserable highways, required centuries, the modern proletarians, thanks to railways, achieve in a few years.

This organization of the proletarians into a class, and consequently into a political party, is continually being upset again by the competition between the workers themselves. But it ever rises up again, stronger, firmer, mightier. It compels legislative recognition of particular interests of the workers, by taking advantage of the divisions among the bourgeoisie itself. Thus the ten-hour bill [7] in England was carried.

Altogether, collisions between the classes of the old society further the course of development of the proletariat in many ways. The bourgeoisie finds itself involved in a constant battle. At first with the aristocracy; later on, with those portions of the bourgeoisie itself whose interests have become antagonistic to the progress of industry; at all times with the bourgeoisie of foreign countries. In all these battles it sees itself compelled to appeal to the proletariat,

[7] The Ten Hours Act, which was passed by Parliament in 1847, in effect limited the working day of all factory workers to ten hours.

to ask for its help, and thus, to drag it into the political arena. The bourgeoisie itself, therefore, supplies the proletariat with its own elements of political and general education, in other words, it furnishes the proletariat with weapons for fighting the bourgeoisie.

Further, as we have already seen, entire sections of the ruling classes are, by the advance of industry, precipitated into the proletariat, or are at least threatened in their conditions of existence. These also supply the proletariat with fresh elements of enlightenment and progress.

Finally, in times when the class struggle nears the decisive hour, the process of dissolution going on within the ruling class, in fact within the whole range of old society, assumes such a violent, glaring character, that a small section of the ruling class cuts itself adrift, and joins the revolutionary class, the class that holds the future in its hands. Just as, therefore, at an earlier period, a section of the nobility went over to the bourgeoisie, so now a portion of the bourgeoisie goes over to the proletariat, and in particular, a portion of the bourgeois ideologists, who have raised themselves to the level of comprehending theoretically the historical movement as a whole.

Of all the classes that stand face to face with the bourgeoisie today, the proletariat alone is a really revolutionary class. The other classes decay and finally disappear in the face of modern industry; the proletariat is its special and essential product.

The lower middle class, the small manufacturer, the shopkeeper, the artisan, the peasant, all these fight against the bourgeoisie, to save from extinction their existence as fractions of the middle class. They are therefore not revolutionary, but conservative. Nay more, they are reactionary, for they try to roll back the wheel of history. If by chance they are revolutionary, they are so only in view of their impending transfer into the proletariat; they thus defend not their present, but their future interests; they desert their own standpoint to adopt that of the proletariat.

The "dangerous class," the social scum (*Lumpenprole-*

tariat), that passively rotting mass thrown off by the lowest layers of old society, may, here and there, be swept into the movement by a proletarian revolution; its conditions of life, however, prepare it far more for the part of a bribed tool of reactionary intrigue.

The social conditions of the old society no longer exist for the proletariat. The proletarian is without property; his relation to his wife and children has no longer anything in common with bourgeois family relations; modern industrial labor, modern subjection to capital, the same in England as in France, in America as in Germany, has stripped him of every trace of national character. Law, morality, religion, are to him so many bourgeois prejudices, behind which lurk in ambush just as many bourgeois interests.

All the preceding classes that got the upper hand, sought to fortify their already acquired status by subjecting society at large to their conditions of appropriation. The proletarians cannot become masters of the productive forces of society, except by abolishing their own previous mode of appropriation, and thereby also every other previous mode of appropriation. They have nothing of their own to secure and to fortify; their mission is to destroy all previous securities for, and insurances of, individual property,

All previous historical movements were movements of minorities, or in the interest of minorities. The proletarian movement is the self-conscious, independent movement of the immense majority, in the interest of the immense majority. The proletariat, the lowest stratum of our present society, cannot stir, cannot raise itself up, without the whole superincumbent strata of official society being sprung into the air.

Though not in substance, yet in form, the struggle of the proletariat with the bourgeoisie is at first a national struggle. The proletariat of each country must, of course, first of all settle matters with its own bourgeoisie.

In depicting the most general phases of the development of the proletariat, we traced the more or less veiled civil war, raging within existing society, up to the point where that war breaks out into open revolution, and where the violent overthrow of the bourgeoisie lays the foundation for the sway of the proletariat.

Hitherto, every form of society has been based, as we have already seen, on the antagonism of oppressing and oppressed classes. But in order to oppress a class, certain conditions must be assured to it under which it can, at least, continue its slavish existence. The serf, in the period of serfdom, raised himself to membership in the commune, just as the petty bourgeois, under the yoke of feudal absolutism, managed to develop into a bourgeois. The modern laborer, on the contrary, instead of rising with the progress of industry, sinks deeper and deeper below the conditions of existence of his own class. He becomes a pauper, and pauperism develops more rapidly than population and wealth. And here it becomes evident, that the bourgeoisie is unfit any longer to be the ruling class in society, and to impose its conditions of existence upon society as an overriding law. It is unfit to rule because it is incompetent to assure an existence to its slave within his slavery, because it cannot help letting him sink into such a state, that it has to feed him, instead of being fed by him. Society can no longer live under this bourgeoisie, in other words, its existence is no longer compatible with society.

The essential condition for the existence and sway of the bourgeois class, is the formation and augmentation of capital; the condition for capital is wage-labor. Wage-labor rests exclusively on competition between the laborers. The advance of industry, whose involuntary promoter is the bourgeoisie, replaces the isolation of the laborers, due to competition, by their revolutionary combination, due to association. The development of modern industry, therefore, cuts from under its feet the very foundation on which the bourgeoisie produces and appropriates products. What the bourgeoisie therefore produces, above all, are its own gravediggers. Its fall and the victory of the proletariat are equally inevitable.

II

PROLETARIANS AND COMMUNISTS

In what relation do the Communists stand to the proletarians as a whole?

The Communists do not form a separate party opposed to other working-class parties.

They have no interests separate and apart from those of the proletariat as a whole.

They do not set up any sectarian principles of their own, by which to shape and mold the proletarian movement.

The Communists are distinguished from the other working-class parties by this only: 1. In the national struggles of the proletarians of the different countries, they point out and bring to the front the common interests of the entire proletariat, independently of all nationality. 2. In the various stages of development which the struggle of the working class against the bourgeoisie has to pass through, they always and everywhere represent the interests of the movement as a whole.

The Communists, therefore, are on the one hand, practically, the most advanced and resolute section of the working-class parties of every country, that section which pushes forward all others; on the other hand, theoretically, they have over the great mass of the proletariat the advantage of clearly understanding the line of march, the conditions, and the ultimate general results of the proletarian movement.

The immediate aim of the Communists is the same as that of all the other proletarian parties: Formation of the proletariat into a class, overthrow of bourgeois supremacy, conquest of political power by the proletariat.

The theoretical conclusions of the Communists are in no way based on ideas or principles that have been invented, or discovered, by this or that would-be universal reformer.

They merely express, in general terms, actual relations springing from an existing class struggle, from a historical movement going on under our very eyes. The abolition of existing property relations is not at all a distinctive feature of communism.

All property relations in the past have continually been subject to historical change consequent upon the change in historical conditions.

The French Revolution, for example, abolished feudal property in favor of bourgeois property.

The distinguishing feature of communism is not the abolition of property generally, but the abolition of bourgeois property. But modern bourgeois private property is the final and most complete expression of the system of producing and appropriating products that is based on class antagonisms, on the exploitation of the many by the few.

In this sense, the theory of the Communists may be summed up in the single sentence: Abolition of private property.

We Communists have been reproached with the desire of abolishing the right of personally acquiring property as the fruit of a man's own labor, which property is alleged to be the groundwork of all personal freedom, activity and independence.

Hard-won, self-acquired, self-earned property! Do you mean the property of the petty artisan and of the small peasant, a form of property that preceded the bourgeois form? There is no need to abolish that; the development of industry has to a great extent already destroyed it, and is still destroying it daily.

Or do you mean modern bourgeois private property?

But does wage-labor create any property for the laborer? Not a bit. It creates capital, *i.e.*, that kind of property which exploits wage-labor, and which cannot increase except upon condition of begetting a new supply of wage-labor for fresh exploitation. Property, in its present form, is based on the antagonism of capital and wage-labor. Let us examine both sides of this antagonism.

To be a capitalist, is to have not only a purely personal, but a social *status* in production. Capital is a collective product, and only by the united action of many members, nay, in the last resort, only by the united action of all members of society, can it be set in motion.

Capital is therefore not a personal, it is a social, power.

When, therefore, capital is converted into common property, into the property of all members of society, personal property is not thereby transformed into social property. It is only the social character of the property that is changed. It loses its class character.

Let us now take wage-labor.

The average price of wage-labor is the minimum wage, *i.e.*, that quantum of the means of subsistence which is absolutely requisite to keep the laborer in bare existence as a laborer. What, therefore, the wage-laborer appropriates by means of his labor, merely suffices to prolong and reproduce a bare existence. We by no means intend to abolish this personal appropriation of the products of labor, an appropriation that is made for the maintenance and reproduction of human life, and that leaves no surplus wherewith to command the labor of others. All that we want to do away with is the miserable character of this appropriation, under which the laborer lives merely to increase capital, and is allowed to live only insofar as the interest of the ruling class requires it.

In bourgeois society, living labor is but a means to increase accumulated labor. In Communist society, accumulated labor is but a means to widen, to enrich, to promote the existence of the laborer.

In bourgeois society, therefore, the past dominates the present; in Communist society, the present dominates the past. In bourgeois society capital is independent and has individuality, while the living person is dependent and has no individuality.

And the abolition of this state of things is called by the bourgeois, abolition of individuality and freedom! And rightly so. The abolition of bourgeois individuality, bourgeois independence, and bourgeois freedom is undoubtedly aimed at.

By freedom is meant, under the present bourgeois conditions of production, free trade, free selling and buying.

But if selling and buying disappears, free selling and

buying disappears also. This talk about free selling and buying, and all the other "brave words" of our bourgeoisie about freedom in general, have a meaning, if any, only in contrast with restricted selling and buying, with the fettered traders of the Middle Ages, but have no meaning when opposed to the Communist abolition of buying and selling, of the bourgeois conditions of production, and of the bourgeoisie itself.

You are horrified at our intending to do away with private property. But in your existing society, private property is already done away with for nine-tenths of the population; its existence for the few is solely due to its nonexistence in the hands of those nine-tenths. You reproach us, therefore, with intending to do away with a form of property, the necessary condition for whose existence is the nonexistence of any property for the immense majority of society.

In a word, you reproach us with intending to do away with your property. Precisely so; that is just what we intend.

From the moment when labor can no longer be converted into capital, money, or rent, into a social power capable of being monopolized, *i.e.*, from the moment when individual property can no longer be transformed into bourgeois property, into capital, from that moment, you say, individuality vanishes.

You must, therefore, confess that by "individual" you mean no other person than the bourgeois, than the middle-class owner of property. This person must, indeed, be swept out of the way, and made impossible.

Communism deprives no man of the power to appropriate the products of society; all that it does is to deprive him of the power to subjugate the labor of others by means of such appropriation.

It has been objected, that upon the abolition of private property all work will cease, and universal laziness will overtake us.

According to this, bourgeois society ought long ago to have gone to the dogs through sheer idleness; for those of its members who work, acquire nothing, and those who acquire anything, do not work. The whole of this objection is but another expression of the tautology: There can no longer be any wage-labor when there is no longer any capital.

All objections urged against the Communist mode of producing and appropriating material products, have, in the same way, been urged against the Communist modes of producing and appropriating intellectual products. Just as, to the bourgeois, the disappearance of class property is the disappearance of production itself, so the disappearance of class culture is to him identical with the disappearance of all culture.

That culture, the loss of which he laments, is, for the enormous majority, a mere training to act as a machine.

But don't wrangle with us so long as you apply, to our intended abolition of bourgeois property, the standard of your bourgeois notions of freedom, culture, law, etc. Your very ideas are but the outgrowth of the conditions of your bourgeois production and bourgeois property, just as your jurisprudence is but the will of your class made into a law for all, a will whose essential character and direction are determined by the economic conditions of existence of your class.

The selfish misconception that induces you to transform into eternal laws of nature and of reason, the social forms springing from your present mode of production and form of property—historical relations that rise and disappear in the progress of production—this misconception you share with every ruling class that has preceded you. What you see clearly in the case of ancient property, what you admit in the case of feudal property, you are of course forbidden to admit in the case of your own bourgeois form of property.

Abolition of the family! Even the most radical flare up at this infamous proposal of the Communists.

On what foundation is the present family, the bourgeois family, based? On capital, on private gain. In its completely developed form this family exists only among the bourgeoisie. But this state of things finds its complement in the practical absence of the family among the proletarians, and in public prostitution.

The bourgeois family will vanish as a matter of course when its complement vanishes, and both will vanish with the vanishing of capital.

Do you charge us with wanting to stop the exploitation of children by their parents? To this crime we plead guilty.

But, you will say, we destroy the most hallowed of relations, when we replace home education by social.

And your education! Is not that also social, and determined by the social conditions under which you educate, by the intervention of society, direct or indirect, by means of schools, etc.? The Communists have not invented the intervention of society in education; they do but seek to alter the character of that intervention, and to rescue education from the influence of the ruling class.

The bourgeois claptrap about the family and education, about the hallowed co-relation of parent and child, becomes all the more disgusting, the more, by the action of modern industry, all family ties among the proletarians are torn asunder, and their children transformed into simple articles of commerce and instruments of labor.

But you Communists would introduce community of women, screams the whole bourgeoisie in chorus.

The bourgeois sees in his wife a mere instrument of production. He hears that the instruments of production are to be exploited in common, and, naturally, can come to no other conclusion than that the lot of being common to all will likewise fall to the women.

He has not even a suspicion that the real point aimed at is to do away with the status of women as mere instruments of production.

For the rest, nothing is more ridiculous than the virtuous indignation of our bourgeois at the community of women which, they pretend, is to be openly and officially established by the Communists. The Communists have no need to introduce community of women; it has existed almost from time immemorial.

Our bourgeois, not content with having the wives and daughters of their proletarians at their disposal, not to speak of common prostitutes, take the greatest pleasure in seducing each other's wives.

Bourgeois marriage is in reality a system of wives in common and thus, at the most, what the Communists might possibly be reproached with is that they desire to introduce, in substitution for a hypocritically concealed, an openly legalized community of women. For the rest, it is self-evident, that the abolition of the present system of production must bring with it the abolition of the community of women springing from that system, *i.e.*, of prostitution both public and private.

The Communists are further reproached with desiring to abolish countries and nationality.

The workingmen have no country. We cannot take from them what they have not got. Since the proletariat must first of all acquire political supremacy, must rise to be the leading class of the nation, must constitute itself *the* nation, it is, so far, itself national, though not in the bourgeois sense of the word.

National differences and antagonisms between peoples are vanishing gradually from day to day, owing to the development of the bourgeoisie, to freedom of commerce, to the world market, to uniformity in the mode of production and in the conditions of life corresponding thereto.

The supremacy of the proletariat will cause them to vanish still faster. United action, of the leading civilized countries at least, is one of the first conditions for the emancipation of the proletariat.

In proportion as the exploitation of one individual by another is put an end to, the exploitation of one nation by another will also be put an end to. In proportion as the antagonism between classes within the nation vanishes, the hostility of one nation to another will come to an end.

The charges against communism made from a religious, a philosophical, and, generally, from an ideological standpoint, are not deserving of serious examination.

Does it require deep intuition to comprehend that man's ideas, views, and conceptions, in one word, man's consciousness, changes with every change in the conditions of his material existence, in his social relations and in his social life?

What else does the history of ideas prove, than that intellectual production changes its character in proportion as material production is changed? The ruling ideas of each age have ever been the ideas of its ruling class.

When people speak of ideas that revolutionize society, they do but express the fact that within the old society the elements of a new one have been created, and that the dissolution of the old ideas keeps even pace with the dissolution of the old conditions of existence.

When the ancient world was in its last throes, the ancient religions were overcome by Christianity. When Christian ideas succumbed in the eighteenth century to rationalist ideas, feudal society fought its death-battle with the then revolutionary bourgeoisie. The ideas of religious liberty and freedom of conscience, merely gave expression to the sway of free competition within the domain of knowledge.

"Undoubtedly," it will be said, "religion, moral, philosophical and juridical ideas have been modified in the course of historical development. But religion, morality, philosophy, political science, and law, constantly survived this change."

"There are, besides, eternal truths, such as Freedom, Justice, etc., that are common to all states of society. But communism abolishes eternal truths, it abolishes all religion, and all morality, instead of constituting them on a new basis; it therefore acts in contradiction to all past historical experience."

What does this accusation reduce itself to? The history of all past society has consisted in the development of class antagonisms, antagonisms that assumed different forms at different epochs.

But whatever form they may have taken, one fact is common to all past ages, *viz.*, the exploitation of one part of society by the other. No wonder, then, that the social consciousness of past ages, despite all the multiplicity and variety it displays, moves within certain common forms, or general ideas, which cannot completely vanish except with the total disappearance of class antagonisms.

The Communist revolution is the most radical rupture with traditional property relations; no wonder that its development involves the most radical rupture with traditional ideas.

But let us have done with the bourgeois objections to communism.

We have seen above, that the first step in the revolution by the working class, is to raise the proletariat to the position of ruling class, to establish democracy.

The proletariat will use its political supremacy to wrest, by degrees, all capital from the bourgeoisie, to centralize all instruments of production in the hands of the state, *i.e.*, of the proletariat organized as the ruling class; and to increase the total of productive forces as rapidly as possible.

Of course, in the beginning, this cannot be effected except by means of despotic inroads on the rights of property, and on the conditions of bourgeois production; by means of measures, therefore, which appear economically insufficient and untenable, but which, in the course of the movement, outstrip themselves, necessitate further inroads upon the old social order, and are unavoidable as a means of entirely revolutionizing the mode of production.

These measures will of course be different in different countries.

Nevertheless in the most advanced countries, the following will be pretty generally applicable.

1. Abolition of property in land and application of all rents of land to public purposes.

2. A heavy progressive or graduated income tax.

3. Abolition of all right of inheritance.

4. Confiscation of the property of all emigrants and rebels.

5. Centralization of credit in the hands of the state, by means of a national bank with state capital and an exclusive monopoly.

6. Centralization of the means of communication and transport in the hands of the state.

7. Extension of factories and instruments of production owned by the state; the bringing into cultivation of waste lands, and the improvement of the soil generally in accordance with a common plan.

8. Equal obligation of all to work. Establishment of industrial armies, especially for agriculture.

9. Combination of agriculture with manufacturing industries; gradual abolition of the distinction between town and country, by a more equable distribution of the population over the country.

10. Free education for all children in public schools. Abolition of child factory labor in its present form. Combination of education with industrial production, etc.

When, in the course of development, class distinctions have disappeared, and all production has been concentrated in the hands of a vast association of the whole nation, the public power will lose its political character. Political power, properly so called, is merely the organized power of one class for oppressing another. If the proletariat during its contest with the bourgeoisie is compelled, by the force of circumstances, to organize itself as a class; if, by means of a revolution, it makes itself the ruling class, and, as such sweeps away by force the old conditions of production, then it will, along with these conditions, have swept away the conditions for the existence of class antagonisms, and of classes generally, and will thereby have abolished its own supremacy as a class.

In place of the old bourgeois society, with its classes and class antagonisms, we shall have an association, in which the free development of each is the condition for the free development of all.

III

SOCIALIST AND COMMUNIST LITERATURE

1. REACTIONARY SOCIALISM

a. Feudal Socialism

Owing to their historical position, it became the vocation of the aristocracies of France and England to write pamphlets against modern bourgeois society. In the French revolution of July, 1830, and in the English reform agitation, these aristocracies again succumbed to the hateful upstart. Thenceforth, a serious political struggle was altogether out of the question. A literary battle alone remained possible. But even in the domain of literature the old cries of the restoration period[1] had become impossible.

In order to arouse sympathy, the aristocracy was obliged to lose sight, apparently, of its own interests, and to formulate its indictment against the bourgeoisie in the interest of the exploited working class alone. Thus the aristocracy took its revenge by singing lampoons against its new master, and whispering in his ears sinister prophecies of coming catastrophe.

In this way arose feudal socialism: half lamentation, half lampoon; half echo of the past, half menace of the future; at times, by its bitter, witty, and incisive criticism, striking the bourgeoisie to the very heart's core, but always ludicrous in its effect through total incapacity to comprehend the march of modern history.

The aristocracy, in order to rally the people to them, waved the proletarian alms-bag in front for a banner. But the people, as often as it joined them, saw on their hindquarters the old feudal coats of arms, and deserted with loud and irreverent laughter.

[1] [Note by Engels] Not the English Restoration 1660 to 1689, but the French Restoration 1814 to 1830

One section of the French Legitimists, and "Young England," [2] exhibited this spectacle.

In pointing out that their mode of exploitation was different from that of the bourgeoisie, the feudalists forget that they exploited under circumstances and conditions that were quite different, and that are now antiquated. In showing that, under their rule, the modern proletariat never existed, they forget that the modern bourgeoisie is the necessary offspring of their own form of society.

For the rest, so little do they conceal the reactionary character of their criticism, that their chief accusation against the bourgeoisie amounts to this, that under the bourgeois regime a class is being developed, which is destined to cut up root and branch the old order of society.

What they upbraid the bourgeoisie with is not so much that it creates a proletariat, as that it creates a *revolutionary* proletariat.

In political practice, therefore, they join in all coercive measures against the working class; and in ordinary life, despite their high-falutin phrases, they stoop to pick up the golden apples dropped from the tree of industry, and to barter truth, love, and honor for traffic in wool, beetroot-sugar, and potato spirits. [3]

[2] The **Legitimists** were the supporters of the elder branch of the Bourbon royal house as against the Orleanists who favored the younger branch; under the July monarchy they attempted to win popularity with the masses by attacking the mercantile and manufacturing interests which supported Louis Philippe. "Young England" was the name taken by a group of British Conservatives, who, under the leadership of Benjamin Disraeli (1804-1881), attacked the evils of industrialism and advocated social reform in the interests of the peasantry and urban working classes.

[3] [Note by Engels] This applies chiefly to Germany where the landed aristocracy and squirearchy have large portions of their estates cultivated for their own account by stewards, and are, moreover, extensive beetroot-sugar manufacturers and distillers of potato spirits. The wealthier British aristocrats are, as yet, rather above that; but they, too, know how to make up for declining rents by lending their names to floaters of more or less shady joint-stock companies.

As the parson has ever gone hand in hand with the landlord, so has Clerical Socialism with Feudal Socialism.

Nothing is easier than to give Christian asceticism a socialist tinge. Has not Christianity declaimed against private property, against marriage, against the state? Has it not preached in the place of these, charity and poverty, celibacy, and mortification of the flesh, monastic life and Mother Church? Christian socialism[4] is but the holy water with which the priest consecrates the heart-burnings of the aristocrat.

b. Petty Bourgeois Socialism

The feudal aristocracy was not the only class that was ruined by the bourgeoisie, not the only class whose conditions of existence pined and perished in the atmosphere of modern bourgeois society. The medieval burgesses and the small peasant proprietors were the precursors of the modern bourgeoisie. In those countries which are but little developed, industrially and commercially, these two classes still vegetate side by side with the rising bourgeoisie.

In countries where modern civilization has become fully developed, a new class of petty bourgeois has been formed, fluctuating between proletariat and bourgeoisie, and ever renewing itself as a supplementary part of bourgeois society. The individual members of this class, however, are being constantly hurled down into the proletariat by the action of competition, and, as modern industry develops, they even see the moment approaching when they will completely disappear as an independent section of modern society, to be replaced, in manufactures, agriculture, and commerce, by overlookers, bailiffs and shopmen.

In countries, like France, where the peasants constitute far more than half of the population, it was natural that writers who sided with the proletariat against the bour-

---

[4] The reference is to certain Continental Socialists and social reformers who based their social doctrine on Christianity; among them the most prominent was Hugues de Lamennais (1782-1854), French priest and aristocrat

geoisie, should use, in their criticism of the bourgeois regime, the standard of the peasant and petty bourgeois, and from the standpoint of these intermediate classes should take up the cudgels for the working class. Thus arose petty bourgeois socialism. Sismondi [5] was the head of this school, not only in France but also in England.

This school of socialism dissected with great acuteness the contradictions in the conditions of modern production. It laid bare the hypocritical apologies of economists. It proved, incontrovertibly, the disastrous effects of machinery and division of labor; the concentration of capital and land in a few hands; overproduction and crises; it pointed out the inevitable ruin of the petty bourgeois and peasant, the misery of the proletariat, the anarchy in production, the crying inequalities in the distribution of wealth, the industrial war of extermination between nations, the dissolution of old moral bonds, of the old family relations, of the old nationalities.

In its positive aims, however, this form of socialism aspires either to restoring the old means of production and of exchange, and with them the old property relations, and the old society, or to cramping the modern means of production and of exchange within the framework of the old property relations that have been, and were bound to be, exploded by those means. In either case, it is both reactionary and utopian.

Its last words are: Corporate guilds for manufacture; patriarchal relations in agriculture.

Ultimately, when stubborn historical facts had dispersed all intoxicating effects of self-deception, this form of socialism ended in a miserable fit of the blues.

c. German or "True" Socialism

The Socialist and Communist literature of France, a literature that originated under the pressure of a bourgeoisie in power, and that was the expression of the strug-

[5] Jean Charles Leonard de Sismondi (1773-1842), Swiss historian and economist, severely criticized the doctrine of *laisser-faire* and advocated certain limited reforms in the interests of the workers

gle against this power, was introduced into Germany at a time when the bourgeoisie, in that country, had just begun its contest with feudal absolutism.

German philosophers, would-be philosophers, and men of letters eagerly seized on this literature, only forgetting that when these writings immigrated from France into Germany, French social conditions had not immigrated along with them. In contact with German social conditions, this French literature lost all its immediate practical significance, and assumed a purely literary aspect. Thus, to the German philosophers of the eighteenth century, the demands of the first French Revolution were nothing more than the demands of "Practical Reason" in general, and the utterance of the will of the revolutionary French bourgeoisie signified in their eyes the laws of pure will, of will as it was bound to be, of true human will generally.[6]

The work of the German *literati* consisted solely in bringing the new French ideas into harmony with their ancient philosophical conscience, or rather, in annexing the French ideas without deserting their own philosophic point of view.

This annexation took place in the same way in which a foreign language is appropriated, namely by translation.

It is well known how the monks wrote silly lives of Catholic saints *over* the manuscripts on which the classical works of ancient heathendom had been written. The German *literati* reversed this process with the profane French literature. They wrote their philosophical nonsense beneath the French original. For instance, beneath the French criticism of the economic functions of money, they wrote "alienation of humanity," and beneath the French criticism of the bourgeois state, they wrote, "dethronement of the category of the general," and so forth.[7]

[6] Marx and Engels are referring particularly to Immanual Kant (1724-1804), whose *Critique of Practical Reason* they thought reflected the economic immaturity of German capitalism

[7] The terms "alienation of humanity" and "dethronement of the category of the general" are terms which were derived from the philosophy of Hegel by the school of philosophical

The introduction of these philosophical phrases at the back of the French historical criticisms they dubbed "Philosophy of Action," "True Socialism," "German Science of Socialism," "Philosophical Foundation of Socialism," and so on.

The French Socialist and Communist literature was thus completely emasculated. And, since it ceased in the hands of the German to express the struggle of one class with the other, he felt conscious of having overcome "French one-sidedness" and of representing, not true requirements, but the requirements of truth; not the interests of the proletariat, but the interests of human nature, of man in general, who belongs to no class, has no reality, who exists only in the misty realm of philosophical fantasy.

This German socialism, which took its school-boy task so seriously and solemnly, and extolled its poor stock-in-trade in such mountebank fashion, meanwhile gradually lost its pedantic innocence.

The fight of the German and especially of the Prussian bourgeoisie against feudal aristocracy and absolute monarchy, in other words, the liberal movement, became more earnest.

By this, the long-wished-for opportunity was offered to "true" socialism of confronting the political movement with the Socialist demands, of hurling the traditional anathemas against liberalism, against representative government, against bourgeois competition, bourgeois freedom of the press, bourgeois legislation, bourgeois liberty and equality, and of preaching to the masses that they had nothing to gain, and everything to lose, by this bourgeois movement. German socialism forgot, in the nick of time, that the French criticism, whose silly echo it was, presupposed the existence of modern bourgeois society, with its corresponding economic conditions of existence, and the political constitution adapted thereto, the very things whose attainment was the object of the pending struggle in Germany.

Socialists which Marx and Engels are attacking in this passage. Two exponents of this school were Moses Hess (1812-1875) and Karl Gruen (1813-1887).

To the absolute governments with their following of parsons, professors, country squires and officials, it served as a welcome scarecrow against the threatening bourgeoisie.

It was a sweet finish after the bitter pills of floggings and bullets, with which these same governments, just at that time, dosed the risings of the German working class.

While this "true" socialism thus served the governments as a weapon for fighting the German bourgeoisie, it, at the same time, directly represented a reactionary interest, the interest of the German Philistines. In Germany the petty bourgeois class, a relic of the sixteenth century, and since then constantly cropping up again under various forms, is the real social basis of the existing state of things.

To preserve this class, is to preserve the existing state of things in Germany. The industrial and political supremacy of the bourgeoisie threatens it with certain destruction— on the one hand, from the concentration of capital; on the other, from the rise of a revolutionary proletariat. "True" socialism appeared to kill these two birds with one stone. It spread like an epidemic.

The robe of speculative cobwebs, embroidered with flowers of rhetoric, steeped in the dew of sickly sentiment, this transcendental robe in which the German Socialists wrapped their sorry "eternal truths," all skin and bone, served to increase wonderfully the sale of their goods amongst such a public.

And on its part, German socialism recognized, more and more, its own calling as the bombastic representative of the petty bourgeois Philistine.

It proclaimed the German nation to be the model nation, and the German petty Philistine to be the typical man. To every villainous meanness of this model man it gave a hidden, higher, socialistic interpretation, the exact contrary of his real character. It went to the extreme length of directly opposing the "brutally destructive" tendency of communism, and of proclaiming its supreme and impartial contempt of all class struggles. With very few exceptions, all the so-called Socialist and Communist publications that now (1847) circulate in Germany belong to the domain of this foul and enervating literature.

2. CONSERVATIVE OR BOURGEOIS SOCIALISM

A part of the bourgeoisie is desirous of redressing social grievances, in order to secure the continued existence of bourgeois society.

To this section belong economists, philanthropists, humanitarians, improvers of the condition of the working class, organizers of charity, members of societies for the prevention of cruelty to animals, temperance fanatics, hole-and-corner reformers of every imaginable kind. This form of socialism has, moreover, been worked out into complete systems.

We may cite Proudhon's *Philosophy of Poverty* as an example of this form.

The socialistic bourgeois want all the advantages of modern social conditions without the struggles and dangers necessarily resulting therefrom. They desire the existing state of society minus its revolutionary and disintegrating elements. They wish for a bourgeoisie without a proletariat. The bourgeoisie naturally conceives the world in which it is supreme to be the best; and bourgeois socialism develops this comfortable conception into various more or less complete systems. In requiring the proletariat to carry out such a system, and thereby to march straightway into the social New Jerusalem, it but requires in reality, that the proletariat should remain within the bounds of existing society, but should cast away all its hateful ideas concerning the bourgeoisie.

A second and more practical, but less systematic, form of this socialism sought to depreciate every revolutionary movement in the eyes of the working class, by showing that no mere political reform, but only a change in the material conditions of existence, in economic relations, could be of any advantage to them. By changes in the material conditions of existence, this form of socialism, however, by no means understands abolition of the bourgeois relations of production, an abolition that can be effected only by a revolution, but administrative reforms, based on the continued existence of these relations; reforms, therefore, that in no respect affect the relations between capital and labor, but, at the best, lessen the cost, and simplify the administrative work of bourgeois government.

Bourgeois socialism attains adequate expression, when, and only when, it becomes a mere figure of speech.

Free trade: For the benefit of the working class. Protective duties: For the benefit of the working class. Prison reform: For the benefit of the working class. These are the last words and the only seriously meant words of bourgeois socialism.

It is summed up in the phrase: the bourgeois are bourgeois—for the benefit of the working class.

3. Critical-Utopian Socialism and Communism

We do not here refer to that literature which, in every great modern revolution, has always given voice to the demands of the proletariat, such as the writings of Babeuf [8] and others.

The first direct attempts of the proletariat to attain its own ends—made in times of universal excitement, when feudal society was being overthrown—necessarily failed, owing to the then undeveloped state of the proletariat, as well as to the absence of the economic conditions for its emancipation, conditions that had yet to be produced, and could be produced by the impending bourgeois epoch alone. The revolutionary literature that accompanied these first movements of the proletariat had necessarily a reactionary character. It inculcated universal asceticism and social leveling in its crudest form.

The socialist and communist systems properly so called, those of St. Simon,[9] Fourier, Owen and others, spring into

[8] François Noel Babeuf (1760-1797), one of the first Socialist leaders of modern times, was guillotined after the suppression of his "Conspiracy of Equals" in 1796

[9] Claude Henri de Rouvroy, Count de Saint-Simon (1760-1825) advocated an industrial society directed by men of science and organized for the benefit of the poor

existence in the early undeveloped period, described above, of the struggle between proletariat and bourgeoisie (see Section 1. Bourgeois and Proletarians).

The founders of these systems see, indeed, the class antagonisms, as well as the action of the decomposing elements in the prevailing form of society. But the proletariat, as yet in its infancy, offers to them the spectacle of a class without any historical initiative or any independent political movement.

Since the development of class antagonism keeps even pace with the development of industry, the economic situation, as such Socialists find it, does not as yet offer to them the material conditions for the emancipation of the proletariat. They therefore search after a new social science, after new social laws, that are to create these conditions.

Historical action is to yield to their personal inventive action; historically created conditions of emancipation to fantastic ones; and the gradual, spontaneous class organization of the proletariat to an organization of society specially contrived by these inventors. Future history, resolves itself, in their eyes, into the propaganda and the practical carrying out of their social plans.

In the formation of their plans they are conscious of caring chiefly for the interests of the working class, as being the most suffering class. Only from the point of view of being the most suffering class does the proletariat exist for them.

The undeveloped state of the class struggle, as well as their own surroundings, causes Socialists of this kind to consider themselves far superior to all class antagonisms. They went to improve the condition of every member of society, even that of the most favored. Hence, they habitually appeal to society at large, without distinction of class; nay, by preference, to the ruling class. For how can people, when once they understand their system, fail to see in it the best possible plan of the best possible state of society?

Hence, they reject all political, and especially all revolutionary action; they wish to attain their ends by peaceful means, and endeavor, by small experiments, necessarily doomed to failure, and by the force of example, to pave the way for the new social gospel.

Such fantastic pictures of future society, painted at a time when the proletariat is still in a very undeveloped state and has but a fantastic conception of its own position, correspond with the first instinctive yearnings of that class for a general reconstruction of society.

But these socialist and communist writings contain also a critical element. They attack every principle of existing society. Hence they are full of the most valuable materials for the enlightenment of the working class. The practical measures proposed in them—such as the abolition of the distinction between town and country; abolition of the family, of private gain and of the wage-system; the proclamation of social harmony; the conversion of the functions of the state into a mere superintendence of production—all these proposals point solely to the disappearance of class antagonisms which were, at that time, only just cropping up, and which, in these publications, are recognized in their earliest, indistinct, and undefined forms only. These proposals, therefore, are of a purely utopian character.

The significance of critical-utopian socialism and communism bears an inverse relation to historical development. In proportion as the modern class struggle develops and takes definite shape, this fantastic standing apart from the contest, these fantastic attacks on it, lose all practical value and all theoretical justification. Therefore, although the originators of these systems were, in many respects, revolutionary, their disciples have, in every case, formed mere reactionary sects. They hold fast by the original views of their masters, in opposition to the progressive historical development of the proletariat. They, therefore, endeavor, and that consistently, to deaden the class struggle and to reconcile the class antagonisms. They still dream of experimental realization of their social utopias, of founding isolated *phalanstères*, of establishing "Home

Colonies," or setting up a "Little Icaria" [10]—pocket editions of the New Jerusalem—and to realize all these castles in the air, they are compelled to appeal to the feelings and purses of the bourgeois. By degrees they sink into the category of the reactionary conservative Socialists depicted above, differing from these only by more systematic pedantry, and by their fanatical and superstitious belief in the miraculous effects of their social science.

They, therefore, violently oppose all political action on the part of the working class; such action, according to them, can only result from blind unbelief in the new gospel.

The Owenites in England, and the Fourierists in France, respectively, oppose the Chartists [11] and the *Réformistes*. [12]

IV

POSITION OF THE COMMUNISTS IN RELATION TO THE VARIOUS EXISTING OPPOSITION PARTIES

Section II has made clear the relations of the Communists to the existing working-class parties, such as the Chartists in England and the Agrarian Reformers in America. [1]

The Communists fight for the attainment of the im-

[10] [Note by Engels] **Phalanstères** were socialist colonies on the plan of Charles Fourier; **Icaria** was the name given by Cabet to his utopia and, later on, to his American communist colony. "Home Colonies" were what Owen called his communist model societies.

[11] **Chartism** was a radical movement in Britain in the period 1837-1848 which demanded political reforms, such as universal manhood suffrage and vote by secret ballot.

[12] The **Réformistes** were the adherents of the newspaper *La Réforme,* which was published in Paris 1843-1850 and was a center of the republican revolution of 1848.

[1] Agitation among tenant farmers in New York State led to the formation of the National Reform Association in 1845 which was the legal cover for a secret society called Young America and which demanded among other things the nationalization of land and the limitation of farms to 160 acres.

mediate aims, for the enforcement of the momentary interests of the working class; but in the movement of the present, they also represent and take care of the future of that movement. In France the Communists ally themselves with the Social-Democrats,[2] against the conservative and radical bourgeoisie, reserving, however, the right to take up a critical position in regard to phrases and illusions traditionally handed down from the great Revolution.

In Switzerland they support the Radicals, without losing sight of the fact that this party consists of antagonistic elements, partly of Democratic Socialists, in the French sense, partly of radical bourgeois.

In Poland they support the party that insists on an agrarian revolution as the prime condition for national emancipation, that party which fomented the insurrection of Cracow in 1846.

In Germany they fight with the bourgeoisie whenever it acts in a revolutionary way, against the absolute monarchy, the feudal squirearchy, and the petty bourgeoisie.

But they never cease, for a single instant, to instill into the working class the clearest possible recognition of the hostile antagonism between bourgeoisie and proletariat, in order that the German workers may straightway use, as so many weapons against the bourgeoisie, the social and political conditions that the bourgeoisie must necessarily introduce along with its supremacy, and in order that, after the fall of the reactionary classes in Germany, the fight against the bourgeoisie itself may immediately begin.

The Communists turn their attention chiefly to Germany, because that country is on the eve of a bourgeois revolution that is bound to be carried out under more advanced conditions of European civilization and with a much more developed proletariat than what existed in

[2] [Note by Engels] The party then represented in Parliament by Ledru-Rollin [Alexander Auguste, 1807-1874], in literature by Louis Blanc [1811-1882], in the daily press by the *Réforme*. The name of social-democracy signified, with these its inventors, a section of the democratic or republican party more or less tinged with socialism.

England in the 17th and in France in the 18th century, and because the bourgeois revolution in Germany will be but the prelude to an immediately following proletarian revolution.

In short, the Communists everywhere support every revolutionary movement against the existing social and political order of things.

In all these movements they bring to the front, as the leading question in each case, the property question, no matter what its degree of development at the time.

Finally, they labor everywhere for the union and agreement of the democratic parties of all countries.

The Communists disdain to conceal their views and aims. They openly declare that their ends can be attained only by the forcible overthrow of all existing social conditions. Let the ruling classes tremble at a Communist revolution. The proletarians have nothing to lose but their chains. They have a world to win.

Workingmen of all countries, unite!

THE EIGHTEENTH BRUMAIRE OF LOUIS BONAPARTE [1]

By KARL MARX

I

HEGEL says somewhere that all great historic facts and personages recur twice. He forgot to add: "Once as tragedy, and again as farce." Caussidière for Danton, Louis Blanc for Robespierre, the "Mountain" of 1848-51 for the "Mountain" of 1793-95, the Nephew for the Uncle.[2] The identical caricature marks also the conditions

[1] On the 9th of November 1799—the 18th Brumaire of the Year VIII in the revolutionary calendar—Napoleon Bonaparte overthrew the Directory and founded his military dictatorship, bringing to an end the decade of revolution which began in 1789. On December 2nd, 1851, his nephew, **Louis Bonaparte,** who had been elected president of the republic established by the revolution of 1848, by a *coup d'état* established a dictatorship which led in the next year to the foundation of the Second Empire. In the work from which the following selections are taken, Marx compares the revolution of 1848 with that of 1789 and analyzes the class basis of the struggles of 1848-1851. *The 18th Brumaire* first appeared in 1852 as a series of articles in *Die Revolution,* a monthly journal published in German in New York. The present translation is based on that made in 1897 by Daniel De Leon (1852-1914), an American Marxist and a founder of the I.W.W.

[2] **Marc Caussidière** (1808-1861), a minor personage in the revolution of 1848, was a leader in the street-fighting of February. **Louis Blanc** (1811-1882), a member of the government set up by the February uprising, attempted to give a socialist tinge to its policy, but like Caussidière was forced to flee the country after the proletarian insurrection of June was suppressed. With these men Marx ironically compares the great

under which the second edition of the eighteenth Brumaire is issued.

Man makes his own history, but he does not make it out
of whole cloth; he does not make it out of conditions
chosen by himself, but out of such as he finds close at
hand. The tradition of all past generations weighs like
a nightmare upon the brain of the living. At the very
time when men appear engaged in revolutionizing things
and themselves, in bringing about what never was before,
precisely at such epochs of revolutionary crisis do they
anxiously conjure up into their service the spirits of the
past, assume their names, their battle cries, their costumes
to enact a new historic scene in such time-honored dis-
guise and with such borrowed language. Thus did Luther
masquerade as the Apostle Paul; thus did the revolution of
1789-1814 drape itself alternately as Roman Republic and
as Roman Empire; nor did the revolution of 1848 know
what better to do than to parody at one time the year
1789, at another the revolutionary traditions of 1793-95.
Thus does the beginner, who has acquired a new language, keep on translating it back into his own mother
tongue; only then has he grasped the spirit of the new
language and is able freely to express himself therewith
when he moves in it without recollections of the old, and
has forgotten in its use his own hereditary tongue.

When these historic conjurations of the dead past are
closely observed a striking difference is immediately
noticeable. Camille Desmoulins, Danton, Robespierre, St.
Just, Napoleon, the heroes as well as the parties and the
masses of the old French revolution, achieved in Roman
costumes and with Roman phrases the task of their time:
the emancipation and the establishment of modern bourgeois society. One set knocked to pieces the old feudal
groundwork and mowed down the feudal heads that had

---

radical leaders of the revolution of 1789, **Georges Jacques
Danton** (1759-1794) and **Maximilien de Robespierre** (1758-1794).
The name of "The Mountain," which was given to the deputies
of the extreme Left who occupied raised seats in the National
Convention during the revolution of 1789, was also taken by
the Radical Democrats of 1848-1851.

grown upon it; Napoleon brought about, within France, the conditions under which alone free competition could develop, the partitioned lands be exploited, the nation's unshackled powers of industrial production be utilized; while, beyond the French frontier, he swept away everywhere the establishments of feudality, so far as requisite, to furnish the bourgeois social system of France with fit surroundings of the European Continent, and such as were in keeping with the time. Once the new social establishment was set on foot, the antediluvian giants vanished, and, along with them, the resuscitated Roman world— the Brutuses, Gracchi, Publicolas, the Tribunes, the Senators, and Caesar himself. In its sober reality, bourgeois society had produced its own true interpreters and mouthpieces in the Says, Cousins, Royer-Collards, Benjamin Constants, and Guizots;[2] its real generals sat behind the office desks; and the hog-headed Louis XVIII was its political chief. Wholly absorbed in the production of wealth and in the peaceful fight of competition, this society could no longer understand that the ghosts of the days of Rome had watched over its cradle. And yet, lacking in heroism as bourgeois society is, it nevertheless had stood in need of heroism, of self-sacrifice, of terror, of civil war, and of bloody battlefields to bring it into the world. Its gladiators found in the stern classic traditions of the Roman republic the ideals and the form, the self-deceptions, that they needed in order to conceal from themselves the narrow bourgeois substance of their own struggles, and to keep their passion up to the height of a great historic tragedy. Thus, at another stage of development, a century before, did Cromwell and the English people draw from the Old Testament the language, passions, and illu-

[2] Jean Baptiste Say (1761-1867), economist, popularized the laisser-faire economics of Adam Smith in France. Victor Cousin (1792-1867), philosopher and educational leader; Pierre Paul Royer-Collard (1763-1845), liberal political leader; Benjamin Constant (1767-1830), political philosopher; and François Pierre Guizot (1787-1874), historian and statesman, who was prime minister at the time of the revolution in 1848, were all closely identified with the "July Monarchy" of Louis Philippe.

sions for their own bourgeois revolution. When the real goal was reached, when the remodeling of English society was accomplished, Locke supplanted Habakkuk.

Accordingly, the reviving of the dead in those revolutions served the purpose of glorifying the new struggles, not of parodying the old; it served the purpose of exaggerating to the imagination the given task, not of recoiling from its practical solution; of reviving again the spirit of revolution, not of trotting out its ghost. . . .

The social revolution of the nineteenth century cannot draw its poetry from the past, it can draw that only from the future. It cannot start upon its work before it has stricken off all superstition concerning the past. Former revolutions required historic reminiscences in order to intoxicate themselves with their own content. The revolution of the nineteenth century must let the dead bury their dead in order to achieve its proper content. With the former, the phrase surpasses the content; with the latter, the content surpasses the phrase.

The February revolution was a sudden attack, a taking of the old society by surprise, and the people proclaimed this unexpected stroke a great historical act whereby the new era was opened. On the 2nd of December the February revolution is conjured away by a card-sharper's sleight of hand, and what is seen to be overthrown is no longer the monarchy, but the liberal concessions which had been wrung from it by centuries of struggles. Instead of *society* itself having conquered a new point, only the state appears to have returned to its oldest form, to the simply brazen rule of the sword and the club. Thus, upon the *coup de main* of February, 1848, comes the response of the *coup de tête*[3] of December, 1851. Easy come, easy go. Meanwhile, the interval did not go by unutilized. During the years 1848-1851, French society made up in abbreviated, because revolutionary, method for the lessons and experiences which in a regular, so to speak, textbook development would have had to precede the February revolution, if it was to be more than a disturbance of the surface.

[3] **Coup de main,** sudden attack; **coup de tête,** act of desperation

Society seems to have fallen back behind its point of departure; in truth it must first create for itself the revolutionary point of departure, the situation, the relations, the conditions, under which alone modern revolution becomes serious.

Bourgeois revolutions, like those of the eighteenth century, rush onward rapidly from success to success, their stage effects outbid one another, men and things seem to be set in flaming brilliants, ecstasy is the prevailing spirit; but they are short-lived, they reach their climax speedily, then society relapses into a long fit of nervous reaction before it learns how to appropriate the fruits of its period of feverish excitement. Proletarian revolutions, on the contrary, such as those of the nineteenth century, criticize themselves constantly; constantly interrupt themselves in their own course; come back to what seems to have been accomplished, in order to start over anew; scorn with cruel thoroughness the half measures, weaknesses and meannesses of their first attempts; seem to throw down their adversary only in order to enable him to draw fresh strength from the earth, and again to rise up against them in more gigantic stature; constantly recoil in fear before the undefined monster magnitude of their own objects—until finally that situation is created which renders all retreat impossible, and the conditions themselves cry out:

"Hic Rhodus, hic salta." [4]

The *first period,* from February 24, or the downfall of Louis Philippe, to May 4, 1848, the date of the assembling of the constitutive assembly—the *February period* proper—may be designated as the *prologue* of the revolution. It officially expressed its own character in this, that the government which it improvised declared itself *provisional;* and, like the government, everything that was broached, attempted, or uttered, pronounced itself *provisional.* Nobody and nothing dared to assume the right of permanent existence and of an actual fact. All the ele-

[4] "**Here is Rhodes, leap here!**" The phrase comes from a fable of Aesop in which a boaster is challenged to make good his boast of a great leap he once made in Rhodes.

ments that had prepared or determined the revolution—dynastic opposition, republican bourgeoisie, democratic-republican small traders' class, social-democratic workers—all found provisionally their place in the February *government*.

It could not be otherwise. The February days contemplated originally a reform of the suffrage laws, whereby the area of the politically privileged among the property-holding class was to be extended, while the exclusive rule of the aristocracy of finance was to be overthrown. When, however, it came to a real conflict, when the people mounted the barricades, when the National Guard stood passive, when the army offered no serious resistance, and the monarchy ran away, then the republic seemed to be a matter of course. Each party interpreted it in its own sense. Won, arms in hand, by the proletariat, they put upon it the stamp of their own class, and proclaimed the *social republic*. Thus the general purpose of modern revolutions was indicated, a purpose, however, that stood in most singular contradiction to everything that, with the material at hand, with the stage of enlightenment that the masses had reached, and under existing circumstances and conditions, could be immediately used. On the other hand, the claims of all the other elements, that had co-operated in the revolution of February, were recognized by the lion's share that they received in the government. Hence, in no period do we find a more motley mixture of high-sounding phrases together with actual doubt and helplessness; of more enthusiastic reform aspirations, together with a more slavish adherence to the old routine; more seeming harmony permeating the whole of society together with a deeper alienation of its several elements. While the Parisian proletariat was still gloating over the sight of the great perspective that had disclosed itself to their view, and was indulging in seriously meant discussions over the social problems, the old powers of society had groomed themselves, had gathered together, had deliberated and found an unexpected support in the mass of the nation—the peasants and small traders—all of whom threw themselves on a sudden upon the political stage, after the barriers of the July monarchy had fallen down.

The *second period,* from May 4, 1848, to the end of May, 1849, is the period of the *constitution,* of the *founding of the bourgeois republic.* Immediately after the February days, not only was the dynastic opposition surprised by the republicans, and the republicans by the Socialists, but all France was surprised by Paris. The National Assembly, that met on May 4, 1848, to frame a constitution, was the outcome of the national elections; it represented the nation. It was a living protest against the assumption of the February days, and it was intended to bring the results of the revolution back to bourgeois standards. In vain did the proletariat of Paris, which immediately understood the character of this national assembly, endeavor, a few days after its meeting, on May 15, to deny its existence by force, to dissolve it, to disintegrate once more into its constituent parts the organic form in which the reactionary spirit of the nation threatened the proletariat. As is known, the 15th of May had no other result than that of removing Blanqui[5] and his associates, *i.e.,* the real leaders of the proletarian party, from the public scene for the whole period of the cycle which we are here considering.

Upon the *bourgeois monarchy* of Louis Philippe, only the *bourgeois republic* could follow; that is to say, a limited portion of the bourgeoisie having ruled under the name of the king, now the whole bourgeoisie was to rule under the name of the people. The demands of the Parisian proletariat are utopian tom-fooleries that have to be done away with. To this declaration of the constitutional national assembly, the Paris proletariat answers with the June insurrection, the most colossal event in the history of European civil wars. The bourgeois republic won. On its side stood the aristocracy of finance, the industrial bourgeoisie; the middle class; the small traders' class; the army; the slums, organized as Guarde Mobile; the intellectual celebrities, the parson's class, and the rural popula-

[5] Louis Auguste Blanqui (1805-1881), a Socialist and democrat, had been a principal leader in the February uprising

tion. On the side of the Parisian proletariat stood none but itself. Over 3,000 insurgents were massacred after the victory, 15,000 were transported without trial. With this defeat, the proletariat steps to the background on the revolutionary stage. It always seeks to crowd forward, so soon as the movement seems to acquire new impetus, but with ever weaker effort and ever smaller results. As soon as one of the social strata lying above it gets into revolutionary ferment, the proletariat enters into alliance with it and so shares all the defeats which the several parties successively suffer. But these succeeding blows become ever weaker the more generally they are distributed over the whole surface of society. The more important leaders of the proletariat, in its councils, and the press, fall one after another victims of the courts, and ever more questionable figures step to the front. *It partly throws itself upon doctrinaire experiments, exchange banks and workers' associations; in other words, it goes into movements, in which it gives up the task of revolutionizing the old world with its own large collective weapons and on the contrary, seeks to bring about its emancipation, behind the back of society, in private ways, within the narrow bounds of its own class conditions, and, consequently inevitably fails.* The proletariat seems to be able neither to find again the revolutionary magnitude within itself nor to draw new energy from the newly formed alliances until *all the classes,* with whom it contended in June, shall lie prostrate along with itself. But in all these defeats, the proletariat succumbs at least with the honor that attaches to great historic struggles; not France alone, all Europe trembles before the June earthquake, while the successive defeats inflicted upon the higher classes are bought so easily that they need the brazen exaggeration of the victorious party itself to be at all able to pass muster as an event; and these defeats become more disgraceful the further removed the defeated party stands from the proletariat.

True enough, the defeat of the June insurgents prepared, leveled the ground, upon which the bourgeois republic could be founded and erected; but it, at the same time, showed that there are in Europe other issues besides that of "republic or monarchy." It revealed the fact that there the bourgeois republic meant the unbridled despotism of one class over another. It proved that, with nations enjoying an older civilization, having developed class distinctions, modern conditions of production, an intellectual consciousness, wherein all traditions of old have been dissolved through the work of centuries, that with such countries the republic means only the *political form for the revolution of bourgeois society*, not its *conservative form of existence*, as is the case in the United States of America, where, true enough, the classes already exist, but have not yet acquired permanent character, are in constant flux and reflux, constantly changing their elements and yielding them up to one another; where the modern means of production, instead of coinciding with a stagnant population, rather compensate for the relative scarcity of heads and hands; and, finally, where the feverishly youthful life of material production, which has to appropriate a new world to itself, has so far left neither time nor opportunity to abolish the illusions of old.

All classes and parties joined hands in the June days in a "Party of Order" against the class of the proletariat, which was designated as the *party of anarchy*, of socialism, of communism. They claimed to have "saved" society against the *enemies of society*. They gave out the slogans of the old social order—*Property, Family, Religion, Order* —as the passwords for their army, and cried out to the counter-revolutionary crusaders: "In this sign thou wilt conquer!" From that moment on, so soon as any of the numerous parties, which had marshaled themselves under this sign against the June insurgents, tries, in turn, to take the revolutionary field in the interest of its own class, it goes down in its turn before the cry: "Property, Family, Religion, Order." Thus it happens that "society is saved" as often as the circle of its ruling class is narrowed, as often as a more exclusive interest asserts itself over the general. Every demand for the most simple bourgeois financial reform, for the most ordinary liberalism, for the most commonplace republicanism, for the flattest democracy, is forthwith punished as an "assault upon so-

ciety," and is branded as "socialism." Finally the high
priests of "Religion and Order" themselves are kicked off
their Pythian[6] tripods; are fetched out of their beds in the
dark, hurried into patrol wagons, thrust into jail or sent
into exile; their temple is razed to the ground, their
mouths are sealed, their pen is broken, their law torn to
pieces in the name of Religion, of Family, of Property,
and of Order. Bourgeois fanatics for "Order" are shot
down on their own balconies by drunken soldiers; their
domestic sanctuaries are profaned; and their houses are
bombarded for amusement—all in the name of Property,
of Family, of Religion, and of Order. Finally, the refuse
of bourgeois society constitutes the "holy phalanx of
Order," and the hero Crapulinsky[7] makes his entry into
the Tuileries[8] as the "Savior of Society" . . .

In the previous chapter I have explained the meaning
of the election of December 10.[9] I shall not here return to
it. Suffice it here to say that it was a reaction of the
peasants, who had been expected to pay the costs of the
February revolution, against the other classes of the nation: it was a *reaction of the country against the city*. It
met with great favor among the soldiers, to whom the
republicans of the *National* [10] had brought neither fame
nor funds; among the great bourgeoisie, who hailed Bonaparte as a bridge to the monarchy; and among the proletarians and small traders, who hailed him as a scourge to

[6] The **Pythian** priestess of Apollox at Delphi sat on a tripod
when delivering her oracles
[7] **Crapulinsky,** the main figure of a poem by Heinrich Heine,
"Two Knights." Here Marx uses the name Crapulinsky (from
the French word, *crapule,* meaning gluttony, drunkenness) to
refer to Louis Bonaparte.
[8] **Tuileries,** a palace in Paris, residence of the king or other
head of the state
[9] On December 10th, 1848, Louis Bonaparte was elected President of the new republic by an overwhelming majority against
Cavaignac and Ledru-Rollin
[10] **National,** a Paris newspaper which supported the republican
cause and opposed the Socialists

Cavaignac.[11] I shall later have occasion to enter more closely into the relation of the peasants to the French Revolution.

The epoch between December 20, 1848,[12] and the dissolution of the constitutional assembly in May, 1849, embraces the history of the downfall of the bourgeois republicans. After they had founded a republic for the bourgeoisie, had driven the revolutionary proletariat from the field, and had meanwhile silenced the democratic middle class, they are themselves shoved aside by the mass of the bourgeoisie, who justly appropriate this republic as their property. This bourgeois mass was *royalist*, however. A part thereof, the large landed proprietors, had ruled under the *Restoration*, hence, was *Legitimist*; the other part, the aristocrats of finance and the large industrial capitalists, had ruled under the July monarchy, hence, was *Orleanist*.[13] The high functionaries of the army, of the University, of the church, in the civil service, of the academy and of the press, divided themselves on both sides, although in unequal parts. Here, in the bourgeois republic, that bore neither the name of *Bourbon*, nor of *Orleans*, but the name of *Capital*, they had found the form of government under which they could all rule in common. Already the June insurrection had united them all into a "Party of Order." The next thing to do was to remove the bourgeois republicans who still held the seats in the National Assembly. Brutally had these pure republicans abused their own physical power against the people; in an equally cowardly, low-spirited, disheartened, broken, powerless manner did they yield, now when the issue was the maintenance of their own republicanism and

---

[11] **Louis Eugene Cavaignac** (1802-1857), a leader of the revolution of 1848 and minister of war in charge of the suppression of the June uprising
[12] On this date, Louis Bonaparte appointed his first ministry.
[13] The **Restoration** was the period from the fall of Napoleon in 1814 to the July revolution of 1830. On **Legitimists** and **Orleanists**, see above, p. 34 n.

their own legislative rights against the executive power
and the royalists. I need not here narrate the shameful
history of their dissolution. It was not a downfall, it was
extinction. Their history is at an end for all time. In the
period that follows, they figure, whether within or without
the Assembly, only as memories—memories that seem
again to come to life so soon as the question is again only
about the word "Republic," and as often as the revolutionary conflict threatens to sink down to the lowest level.
In passing, I might observe that the journal which gave
to this party its name, the *National,* goes over to socialism
during the following period. . . .

On May 29, 1849, the legislative National Assembly
convened. On December 2, 1851, it was broken up. This
period embraces the term of life of the *Constitutional* or
Parliamentary Republic.

In the first French revolution, upon the reign of the
Constitutionalists succeeds that of the *Girondins;* and upon
the reign of the *Girondins* follows that of the *Jacobins.*[14]
Each of these parties in succession rests upon its more
advanced element. So soon as it has carried the revolution
far enough not to be able to keep pace with, much less
march ahead of it, it is shoved aside by its more daring
allies, who stand behind it, and it is sent to the guillotine.
Thus the revolution moves along an upward line.

Just the reverse in 1848. The proletarian party appears
as an appendage to the small traders-democratic party; it
is betrayed by the latter and allowed to fall on April 16,
May 15, and in the June days. In its turn, the democratic
party leans upon the shoulders of the bourgeois republicans; barely do the bourgeois republicans believe them-

---

[14] The **Constitutionalists,** who had their center in the club of
the Feuillants, supported the limited monarchy of the constitution of 1791 against both the friends of the absolute monarchy
and the republicans. The **Girondins,** who were given this name
because the leading exponents of their views came from the
Gironde region of France, aided in the fall of the monarchy
in 1792, but were in turn overthrown by the Mountain. The
Jacobins, the most famous of the political clubs, became more
radical in the course of the revolution and emerged as the
focus of the Terror 1793-1794.

selves firmly in power, than they shake off these trouble-
some associates for the purpose of themselves leaning
upon the shoulders of the Party of Order. The Party of
Order draws in its shoulders, lets the bourgeois republicans tumble down heels over head, and throws itself
upon the shoulders of the armed power. Finally, still of
the mind that it is sustained by the shoulders of the
armed power, the Party of Order notices one fine morning
that these shoulders have turned into bayonets. Each party
kicks backward at those that are pushing forward, and
leans forward upon those that are crowding backward;
no wonder that, in this ludicrous posture, each loses its
balance, and, after having made the inevitable grimaces,
collapses with odd capers. Accordingly, the revolution
moves along a downward line. It finds itself in this retreat-
ing motion before the last February-barricade is cleared
away, and the first governmental authority of the revolution has been constituted. . . .

Before we follow this parliamentary history any further,
a few observations are necessary, in order to avoid certain
common deceptions concerning the whole character of
the epoch that lies before us. According to the view of the
democrats, the issue, during the period of the legislative
National Assembly, was, the same as during the period
of the constitutive assembly, simply the struggle between
republicans and royalists; the movement itself was summed
up by them in the catchword *Reaction*—a night, in which
all cats are gray, and which allows them to drawl out their
night-watchman's commonplaces. Indeed, at first sight,
the Party of Order presents the appearance of a tangle of
royalist factions, which not only intrigue against each
other, each aiming to raise its own pretender to the
throne, and exclude the pretender of the opposite party,
but also are all united in a common hatred for and common attacks against the "Republic." On its side, the
Mountain appears, in counter-distinction to the royalist
conspiracy, as the representative of the "Republic." The
Party of Order seems constantly engaged in a "Reaction,"
which, neither more nor less than in Prussia, is directed
against the press, the right of association and the like,

and is enforced by brutal police interventions on the part
of the bureaucracy, the police and the public prosecutor—
just as in Prussia; the Mountain, on the contrary, is engaged with equal assiduity in parrying these attacks, and
thus in defending the "eternal rights of man"—as every
so-called people's party has more or less done for the last
hundred and fifty years. At a closer inspection, however,
of the situation and of the parties, this superficial appearance, which veils the *class struggle,* together with the
peculiar physiognomy of this period, vanishes wholly.

Legitimists and Orleanists constituted, as said before,
the two large factions of the Party of Order. What held
these two factions to their respective pretenders, and in-
versely kept them apart from each other, what else was it
but the lily and the tricolor, the House of Bourbon and
the House of Orleans, different shades of royalty? Was it
the confession of faith of royalism at all? Under the Bourbons, *large landed property* ruled together with its parsons
and lackeys; under the Orleanist, it was high finance,
large industry, large commerce, i.e., *Capital,* with its reti-
nue of lawyers, professors and orators. The Legitimate
Monarchy was but the political expression for the hereditary rule of the landlords, as the July monarchy was but
the political expression for the usurped rule of the bourgeois upstarts. What, accordingly, kept these two factions
apart was no so-called set of principles, it was their material conditions for life—two different sorts of property;
it was the old antagonism of the City and the Country, the
rivalry between capital and landed property. That simultaneously old recollections; personal animosities, fears and
hopes; prejudices and illusions; sympathies and antip-
athies; convictions, faith and principles bound these factions to one house or the other, who denies it? Upon the
several forms of property, upon the social conditions of
existence, a whole superstructure is reared of various and
peculiarly shaped feelings, illusions, habits of thought, and
conceptions of life. The whole class produces and shapes
these out of its material foundation and out of the corresponding social conditions. The individual unit to whom
they flow through tradition and education may fancy that

they constitute the true reasons for and premises of his conduct. Although Orleanists and Legitimists, each of these factions, sought to make itself and the other believe that what kept the two apart was the attachment of each to its respective royal house; nevertheless, facts proved later that it rather was their divided interest that forbade the union of the two royal houses. As, in private life, the distinction is made between what a man thinks of himself and says, and that which he really is and does, so, all the more, must the phrases and notions of parties in historic struggles be distinguished from their real organism and their real interests, their conceptions from their reality. Orleanists and Legitimists found themselves in the republic beside each other with equal claims. Each side wishing, in opposition to the other, to carry out the *restoration* of its *own* royal house, meant nothing else than that each of the two great *Interests* into which the bourgeoisie is divided—land and capital—sought to restore its own supremacy and the subordination of the other. We speak of two bourgeois interests because large landed property, despite its feudal coquetry and pride of race, has become completely bourgeois through the development of modern society. Thus did the Tories of England long fancy that they were enthusiastic for the Kingdom, the Church and the beauties of the old English Constitution, until the day of danger wrung from them the admission that their enthusiasm was only for *Ground-Rent*. . . .

Against the coalition of the bourgeoisie, a coalition was made between the small traders and the workingmen— the so-called *Social Democratic* Party. The small traders found themselves ill rewarded after the June days of 1848; they saw their material interests endangered, and the democratic guarantees, that were to uphold their interests, made doubtful. Hence, they drew closer to the workingmen. On the other hand, their parliamentary representatives—the *Mountain*—after being shoved aside during the dictatorship of the bourgeois republicans, had, during the last half of the term of the constitutive convention, regained their lost popularity through the struggle with Bonaparte and the royalist ministers. They had made an alliance with the Socialist leaders. During February, 1849, reconciliation banquets were held. A common program was drafted, joint election committees were empaneled, and fusion candidates were set up. The revolutionary point was thereby broken off the social demands of the proletariat, and a democratic turn given to them; while, from the democratic claims of the small traders' class, the mere political form was stripped off and the socialist point was pushed forward. Thus arose *Social Democracy*. The new *Mountain*, the result of this combination, contained, with the exception of some figures from the working class and some Socialist sectarians, the identical elements of the old Mountain, only numerically stronger. In the course of events it had, however, changed, together with the class that it represented. The peculiar character of the Social Democracy is summed up in this: that democratic-republican institutions are demanded as the means, not to remove the two extremes—Capital and Wage-slavery—but in order to weaken their antagonism and transform them into a harmonious whole. However different the methods may be that are proposed for the accomplishment of this object, however much the object itself may be festooned with more or less revolutionary fancies, the substance remains the same. This substance is the transformation of society upon democratic lines, but a transformation within the boundaries of the small traders' class. Only one must not form the narrow-minded notion that the small traders' class means on principle to enforce a selfish class interest. It believes rather that the *special* conditions for its own emancipation are the *general* conditions under which alone modern society can be saved and the class struggle avoided. Just as little must one suppose that the democratic representatives are all shopkeepers or their enthusiastic supporters. They may—by education and individual standing—be as distant from them as heaven is from earth. That which makes them representatives of the small traders' class is that they do not intellectually leap the bounds which that class itself does not leap in practical life; that, consequently, they are theoretically driven to the same problems and solutions, to which material interests and social standing practically drive the latter. Such, in fact, is at all times the relation of the *political* and the *literary* representatives of a class to the class they represent. . . .

As the Bourbons are the dynasty of large landed property, as the Orleans are the dynasty of money, so are the Bonapartes the dynasty of the peasants, that is, of the mass of the French people. Not the Bonaparte who threw himself at the feet of the bourgeois parliament, but the Bonaparte, who swept away the bourgeois parliament, is the elect of the peasants. For three years the cities had succeeded in falsifying the meaning of the election of December 10, and in cheating the peasant out of the restoration of the Empire. The election of December 10, 1848, is not carried out until the *coup d'état* of December 2, 1851.

The small peasants form a huge mass, whose members live in similar conditions without, however, entering into many and varied relations with one another. Their method of production isolates them from one another, instead of drawing them into mutual intercourse. This isolation is promoted by the poor means of communication in France, together with the poverty of the peasants themselves. Their field of production, the small holding, admits of no division of labor in its cultivation and no application of science; hence, no variety of development, diversity of talents, no wealth of social relations. Every individual peasant family is almost self-sufficient; it itself produces directly the greater part of what it consumes; and so earns its livelihood more by means of an interchange with nature than by intercourse with society. The small holding, the peasant and his family; alongside them another small holding, another peasant and another family. A few score of these make up a village, and a few score of villages make up a department. Thus the great mass of the French nation is constituted by the simple addition of similar magnitudes—much as potatoes in a sack form a sackful of potatoes. Insofar as millions of families live under economic conditions that separate their mode of life, their interests and their culture from those of the other classes, and that place them in an attitude hostile toward the latter, they constitute a class; insofar as there exists only a local connection among these peasants, a connection which the individuality and exclusiveness of their interests prevent from generating among them any unity of interest, national connections, and political organization, they do not constitute a class. Consequently, they are unable to assert their class interests in their own name, be it by a parliament or by convention. They cannot represent one another, they must themselves be represented. Their representative must at the same time appear as their master, as an authority over them, as an unlimited governmental power, that protects them from above, bestows rain and sunshine upon them. Accordingly, the political influence of the small peasant finds its ultimate expression in an executive power that subjugates the society to its own autocratic will.

THE GENERAL LAW OF CAPITALIST ACCUMULATION[1]

By KARL MARX

Section 1.—THE INCREASED DEMAND FOR LABOR-POWER THAT ACCOMPANIES ACCUMULATION, THE COMPOSITION OF CAPITAL REMAINING THE SAME.

IN THIS chapter we consider the influence of the growth of capital on the lot of the laboring class. The most important factor in this inquiry, is the composition of capital and the changes it undergoes in the course of the process of accumulation.

The composition of capital is to be understood in a twofold sense. On the side of value, it is determined by the proportion in which it is divided into constant capital or value of the means of production, and variable capital or value of labor-power, the sum total of wages. On the side of material, as it functions in the process of production, all capital is divided into means of production and living labor-power. This latter composition is determined by the relation between the mass of the means of production employed, on the one hand, and the mass of labor necessary for their employment on the other. I call the former the *value composition*, the latter the *technical composition* of capital. Between the two there is a strict correlation. To express this, I call the value-composition of capital, insofar as it is determined by its technical composition and mirrors the changes of the latter, the *organic composition*

[1] These selections are from Sections 1-4 of Chapter 25 of the first English edition of Volume I of *Capital*, translated from the 3rd German edition by Samuel Moore and Dr. E. Aveling, edited by Friedrich Engels and published in 1886.

of capital. Wherever I refer to the composition of capital, without further qualification, its organic composition is always understood.

The many individual capitals invested in a particular branch of production have, one with another, more or less different compositions. The average of their individual compositions gives us the composition of the total capital in this branch of production. Lastly, the average of these averages, in all branches of production, gives us the composition of the total social capital of a country, and with this alone are we, in the last resort, concerned in the following investigation.

Growth of capital involves growth of its variable constituent or of the part invested in labor-power. A part of the surplus-value turned into additional capital must always be retransformed into variable capital, or additional labor-fund. If we suppose that, all other circumstances remaining the same, the composition of capital also remains constant (*i.e.*, that a definite mass of means of production constantly needs the same mass of labor-power to set in motion), then the demand for labor and the subsistence-fund of the laborers clearly increase in the same proportion as the capital, and the more rapidly, the more rapidly the capital increases. Since the capital produces yearly a surplus-value, of which one part is yearly added to the original capital; since this increment itself grows yearly along with the augmentation of the capital already functioning; since lastly, under special stimulus to enrichment, such as the opening of new markets, or of new spheres for the outlay of capital in consequence of newly developed social wants, &c., the scale of accumulation may be suddenly extended, merely by a change in the division of the surplus value or surplus product into capital and revenue, the requirements of accumulating capital may exceed the increase of labor-power or of the number of laborers; the demand for laborers may exceed the supply, and, therefore, wages may rise. This must, indeed, ultimately be the case if the conditions supposed above continue. For since in each year more laborers are employed than in its predecessor, sooner or later a point must be reached, at which the requirements of accumulation begin to surpass the customary supply of labor, and, therefore, a rise of wages takes place. A lamentation on this score was heard in England during the whole of the fifteenth, and the first half of the eighteenth centuries. The more or less favorable circumstances in which the wage-working class supports and multiplies itself, in no way alter the fundamental character of capitalist production. As simple reproduction constantly reproduces the capital-relation itself, *i.e.*, the relation of capitalists on the one hand, and wage-workers on the other, so reproduction on a progressive scale, *i.e.*, accumulation, reproduces the capital relation on a progressive scale, more capitalists or larger capitalists at this pole, more wage-workers at that. The reproduction of a mass of labor-power, which must incessantly reincorporate itself with capital for that capital's self-expansion; which cannot get free from capital, and whose enslavement to capital is only concealed by the variety of individual capitalists to whom it sells itself, this reproduction of labor-power forms, in fact, an essential of the reproduction of capital itself. Accumulation of capital is, therefore, increase of the proletariat. . . .

Under the conditions of accumulation supposed thus far, which conditions are those most favorable to the laborers, their relation of dependence upon capital takes 'on a form endurable, or, as Eden says: "easy and liberal." [2] Instead of becoming more intensive with the growth of capital, this relation of dependence only becomes more extensive, *i.e.*, the sphere of capital's exploitation and rule merely extends with its own dimensions and the number of its subjects. A larger part of their own surplus product, always increasing and continually transformed into additional capital, comes back to them in the shape of means of payment, so that they can extend the circle of their enjoyments; can make some additions to their consumption-fund of clothes, furniture, &c., and can lay by small reserve-funds of money. But just as little as better clothing, food, and treatment, and a larger peculium, do away with

[2] Sir F. M. Eden, eighteenth-century economist and disciple of Adam Smith.

the exploitation of the slave, so little do they set aside that of the wage-worker. A rise in the price of labor, as a consequence of accumulation of capital, only means, in fact, that the length and weight of the golden chain the wage-worker has already forged for himself, allow of a relaxation of the tension of it. In the controversies on this subject the chief fact has generally been overlooked, viz., the *differentia specifica*[3] of capitalistic production. Labor-power is sold today, not with a view of satisfying, by its service or by its product, the personal needs of the buyer. His aim is augmentation of his capital, production of commodities containing more labor than he pays for, containing therefore a portion of value that costs him nothing, and that is nevertheless realized when the commodities are sold. Production of surplus-value is the absolute law of this mode of production. Labor-power is only salable so far as it preserves the means of production in their capacity of capital, reproduces its own value as capital, and yields in unpaid labor a source of additional capital. The conditions of its sale, whether more or less favorable to the laborer, include therefore the necessity of its constant re-selling, and the constantly extended reproduction of all wealth in the shape of capital. Wages, as we have seen, by their very nature, always imply the performance of a certain quantity of unpaid labor on the part of the laborer. Altogether, irrespective of the case of a rise of wages with a falling price of labor, &c., such an increase only means at best a quantitative diminution of the unpaid labor that the worker has to supply. This diminution can never reach the point at which it would threaten the system itself. Apart from violent conflicts as to the rate of wages (and Adam Smith has already shown that in such a conflict, taken on the whole, the master is always master), a rise in the price of labor resulting from accumulation of capital implies the following alternative:

Either the price of labor keeps on rising, because its rise does not interfere with the progress of accumulation. In

---

[3] **differentia specifica,** distinguishing characteristic

this there is nothing wonderful, for, says Adam Smith,[4] "after these (profits) are diminished, stock may not only continue to increase, but to increase much faster than before. . . . A great stock, though with small profits, generally increases faster than a small stock with great profits." In this case it is evident that a diminution in the unpaid labor in no way interferes with the extension of the domain of capital.—Or, on the other hand, accumulation slackens in consequence of the rise in the price of labor, because the stimulus of gain is blunted. The rate of accumulation lessens; but with its lessening, the primary cause of that lessening vanishes, *i.e.*, the disproportion between capital and exploitable labor-power. The mechanism of the process of capitalist production removes the very obstacles that it temporarily creates. The price of labor falls again to a level corresponding with the needs of the self-expansion of capital, whether the level be below, the same as, or above the one which was normal before the rise of wages took place. We see thus: In the first case, it is not the diminished rate either of the absolute, or of the proportional, increase in labor-power, or laboring population, which causes capital to be in excess, but conversely the excess of capital that makes exploitable labor-power insufficient. In the second case, it is not the increased rate either of the absolute, or of the proportional, increase in labor-power, or laboring population, that makes capital insufficient; but, conversely, the relative diminution of capital that causes the exploitable labor-power, or rather its price, to be in excess. It is these absolute movements of the accumulation of capital which are reflected as relative movements of the mass of exploitable labor-power, and therefore seem produced by the latter's own independent movement. To put it mathematically: the rate of accumulation is the independent, not the dependent, variable; the rate of wages, the dependent, not the independent, variable. Thus, when the industrial cycle is in the phase of crisis, a general fall in the price of commodities

[4] Adam Smith, *The Wealth of Nations* (Aberdeen, 1848), Vol. II, p. 189

is expressed as a rise in the value of money, and, in the phase of prosperity, a general rise in the price of commodities, as a fall in the value of money. The so-called currency school concludes from this that with high prices too little, with low prices too much money is in circulation. Their ignorance and complete misunderstanding of facts are worthily paralleled by the economists, who interpret the above phenomena of accumulation by saying that there are now too few, now too many wage laborers.

The law of capitalist production, that is at the bottom of the pretended "natural law of population," reduces itself simply to this: The correlation between accumulation of capital and rate of wages is nothing else than the correlation between the unpaid labor transformed into capital, and the additional paid labor necessary for the setting in motion of this additional capital. It is therefore in no way a relation between two magnitudes, independent one of the other: on the one hand, the magnitude of the capital; on the other, the number of the laboring population; it is rather, at bottom, only the relation between the unpaid and the paid labor of the same laboring population. If the quantity of unpaid labor supplied by the working-class, and accumulated by the capitalist class, increases so rapidly that its conversion into capital requires an extraordinary addition of paid labor, then wages rise, and, all other circumstances remaining equal, the unpaid labor diminishes in proportion. But as soon as this diminution touches the point at which the surplus-labor that nourishes capital is no longer supplied in normal quantity, a reaction sets in: a smaller part of revenue is capitalized, accumulation lags, and the movement of rise in wages receives a check. The rise of wages therefore is confined within limits that not only leave intact the foundations of the capitalistic system, but also secure its reproduction on a progressive scale. The law of capitalistic accumulation, metamorphosed by economists into a pretended law of nature, in reality merely states that the very nature of accumulation excludes every diminution in the degree of exploitation of labor, and every rise in the price of labor, which could seriously imperil the continual reproduction, on an ever enlarging scale, of the capitalistic relation. It cannot be otherwise in a mode of production in which the laborer exists to satisfy the needs of self-expansion of existing values, instead of on the contrary, material wealth existing to satisfy the needs of development on the part of the laborer. As, in religion, man is governed by the products of his own brain, so in capitalistic production, he is governed by the products of his own hand.

Section 2.—RELATIVE DIMINUTION OF THE VARIABLE PART OF CAPITAL SIMULTANEOUSLY WITH THE PROGRESS OF ACCUMULATION AND OF THE CONCENTRATION THAT ACCOMPANIES IT.

According to the economists themselves, it is neither the actual extent of social wealth, nor the magnitude of the capital already functioning, that lead to a rise of wages, but only the constant growth of accumulation and the degree of rapidity of that growth. (Adam Smith, Book I, chapter 8.) So far, we have only considered one special phase of this process, that in which the increase of capital occurs along with a constant technical composition of capital. But the process goes beyond this phase.

Once given the general basis of the capitalistic system, then, in the course of accumulation, a point is reached at which the development of the productivity of social labor becomes the most powerful lever of accumulation. "The same cause," says Adam Smith, "which raises the wages of labor, the increase of stock, tends to increase its productive powers, and to make a smaller quantity of labor produce a greater quantity of work."

Apart from natural conditions, such as fertility of the soil, &c., and from the skill of independent and isolated producers (shown rather qualitatively in the goodness than quantitatively in the mass of their products), the degree of productivity of labor, in a given society, is expressed in the relative extent of the means of production that one laborer, during a given time, with the same tension of labor-power, turns into products. The mass of the means of production which he thus transforms, increases with the productiveness of his labor. But those means of production play a double part. The increase of some is a consequence, that of the others a condition of the increasing productivity of labor. *E.g.*, with the division of labor in manufacture, and with the use of machinery, more raw material is worked up in the same time, and, therefore, a greater mass of raw material and auxiliary substances enter into the labor-process. That is the consequence of the increasing productivity of labor. On the other hand, the mass of machinery, beasts of burden, mineral manures, drainpipes, &c., is a condition of the increasing productivity of labor. So also is it with the means of production concentrated in buildings, furnaces, means of transport, &c. But whether condition or consequence, the growing extent of the means of production, as compared with the labor-power incorporated with them, is an expression of the growing productiveness of labor. The increase of the latter appears, therefore, in the diminution of the mass of labor in proportion to the mass of means of production moved by it, or in the diminution of the subjective factor of the labor process as compared with the objective factor.

This change in the technical composition of capital, this growth in the mass of means of production, as compared with the mass of the labor-power that vivifies them, is reflected again in its value-composition, by the increase of the constant constituent of capital at the expense of its variable constituent. There may be, *e.g.*, originally 50 per cent of a capital laid out in means of production, and 50 per cent in the labor-power; later on, with the development of the productivity of labor, 80 per cent in means of production, 20 per cent in labor-power, and so on. This law of the progressive increase in constant capital, in proportion to the variable, is confirmed at every step (as already shown) by the comparative analysis of the prices of commodities, whether we compare different economic epochs or different nations in the same epoch. The relative magnitude of the element of price, which represents the value of the means of production only, or the constant part of capital consumed, is in direct, the relative magnitude of the other element of price that pays labor (the variable part of capital) is in inverse proportion to the advance of accumulation.

This diminution in the variable part of capital as compared with the constant, or the altered value-composition of the capital, however, only shows approximately the change in the composition of its material constituents. If, e.g., the capital-value employed today in spinning is $\frac{7}{8}$ constant and $\frac{1}{8}$ variable, whilst at the beginning of the eighteenth century it was $\frac{1}{2}$ constant and $\frac{1}{2}$ variable, on the other hand, the mass of raw material, instruments of labor, &c., that a certain quantity of spinning labor consumes productively today, is many hundred times greater than at the beginning of the eighteenth century. The reason is simply that, with the increasing productivity of labor, not only does the mass of the means of production consumed by it increase, but their value compared with their mass diminishes. Their value therefore rises absolutely, but not in proportion to their mass. The increase of the difference between constant and variable capital is, therefore, much less than that of the difference between the mass of the means of production into which the constant, and the mass of the labor-power into which the variable, capital is converted. The former difference increases with the latter, but in a smaller degree.

But, if the progress of accumulation lessens the relative magnitude of the variable part of capital, it by no means, in doing this, excludes the possibility of a rise in its absolute magnitude. Suppose that a capital-value at first is divided into 50 per cent of constant and 50 per cent of variable capital; later into 80 per cent of constant and 20 per cent of variable. If in the meantime the original capital, say £6,000, has increased to £18,000, its variable constituent has also increased. It was £3,000, it is now £3,600. But whereas formerly an increase of capital by 20 per cent would have sufficed to raise the demand for labor 20 per cent, now this latter rise requires a tripling of the original capital.

In Part IV[1] it was shown, how the development of the

[1] Part IV is entitled "Production of Relative Surplus Value"; in it Marx discusses how surplus value is increased, not through

productiveness of social labor presupposes co-operation on a large scale; how it is only upon this supposition that division and combination of labor can be organized, and the means of production economized by concentration on a vast scale; how instruments of labor which, from their very nature, are only fit for use in common, such as a system of machinery, can be called into being; how huge natural forces can be pressed into the service of production; and how the transformation can be effected of the process of production into a technological application of science. On the basis of the production of commodities, where the means of production are the property of private persons, and where the artisan therefore either produces commodities, isolated from and independent of others, or sells his labor-power as a commodity, because he lacks the means for independent industry, co-operation on a large scale can realize itself only in the increase of individual capitals, only in proportion as the means of social production and the means of subsistence are transformed into the private property of capitalists. The basis of the production of commodities can admit of production on a large scale in the capitalistic form alone. A certain accumulation of capital, in the hands of individual producers of commodities, forms therefore the necessary preliminary of the specifically capitalistic mode of production. We had, therefore, to assume that this occurs during the transition from handicraft to capitalistic industry. It may be called primitive accumulation, because it is the historic basis, instead of the historic result of specifically capitalist production. How it itself originates, we need not here inquire as yet. It is enough that it forms the starting point. But all methods for raising the social productive power of labor that are developed on this basis, are at the same time methods for the increased production of surplus-value or surplus-product, which in its turn is the formative

a lengthening of the working day, but by an increase in productivity which by reducing the amount of labor needed to produce what is necessary for the worker's subsistence makes it possible for the capitalist to take a larger share of the value created by labor element of accumulation. They are, therefore, at the same time methods of the production of capital by capital, or methods of its accelerated accumulation. The continual retransformation of surplus-value into capital now appears in the shape of the increasing magnitude of the capital that enters into the process of production. This in turn is the basis of an extended scale of production, of the methods for raising the productive power of labor that accompany it, and of accelerated production of surplus-value. If, therefore, a certain degree of accumulation of capital appears as a condition of the specifically capitalist mode of production, the latter causes conversely an accelerated accumulation of capital. With the accumulation of capital, therefore, the specifically capitalistic mode of production develops, and with the capitalist mode of production the accumulation of capital. Both these economic factors bring about, in the compound ratio of the impulses they reciprocally give one another, that change in the technical composition of capital by which the variable constituent becomes always smaller and smaller as compared with the constant.

Every individual capital is a larger or smaller concentration of means of production, with a corresponding command over a larger or smaller labor-army. Every accumulation becomes the means of new accumulation. With the increasing mass of wealth which functions as capital, accumulation increases the concentration of that wealth in the hands of individual capitalists, and thereby widens the basis of production on a large scale and of the specific methods of capitalist production. The growth of social capital is effected by the growth of many individual capitals. All other circumstances remaining the same, individual capitals, and with them the concentration of the means of production, increase in such proportion as they form aliquot parts of the total social capital. At the same time portions of the original capitals disengage themselves and function as new independent capitals. Besides other causes, the division of property, within capitalist families, plays a great part in this. With the accumulation of capital, therefore, the number of capitalists grows to a greater or less extent. Two points characterize this kind of concentration which grows directly out of, or rather is identical with, accumulation. First: The increasing concentration of the social means of production in the hands of individual capitalists is, other things remaining equal, limited by the degree of increase of social wealth. Second: The part of social capital domiciled in each particular sphere of production is divided among many capitalists who face one another as independent commodity-producers competing with each other. Accumulation and the concentration accompanying it are, therefore, not only scattered over many points, but the increase of each functioning capital is thwarted by the formation of new and the subdivision of old capitals. Accumulation, therefore, presents itself on the one hand as increasing concentration of the means of production, and of the command over labor; on the other, as repulsion of many individual capitals one from another.

This splitting-up of the total social capital into many individual capitals or the repulsion of its fractions one from another, is counteracted by their attraction. This last does not mean that simple concentration of the means of production and of the command over labor, which is identical with accumulation. It is concentration of capitals already formed, destruction of their individual independence, expropriation of capitalist by capitalist, transformation of many small into few large capitals. This process differs from the former in this, that it only presupposes a change in the distribution of capital already to hand, and functioning; its field of action is therefore not limited by the absolute growth of social wealth, by the absolute limits of accumulation. Capital grows in one place to a huge mass in a single hand, because it has in another place been lost by many. This is centralization proper, as distinct from accumulation and concentration.

The laws of this centralization of capitals, or of the attraction of capital by capital, cannot be developed here. A brief hint at a few facts must suffice. The battle of competition is fought by cheapening of commodities. The cheapness of commodities depends, *cæteris paribus*, on the productiveness of labor, and this again on the scale of production. Therefore, the larger capitals beat the smaller. It will further be remembered that, with the development of the capitalist mode of production, there is an increase in the minimum amount of individual capital necessary to carry on a business under its normal conditions. The smaller capitals, therefore, crowd into spheres of production which modern industry has only sporadically or incompletely got hold of. Here competition rages in direct proportion to the number, and in inverse proportion to the magnitudes, of the antagonistic capitals. It always ends in the ruin of many small capitalists, whose capitals partly pass into the hand of their conquerors, partly vanish. Apart from this, with capitalist production an altogether new force comes into play—the credit system. Not only is this itself a new and mighty weapon in the battle of competition. By unseen threads it, moreover, draws the disposable money, scattered in larger or smaller masses over the surface of society, into the hands of individual or associated capitalists. It is the specific machine for the centralization of capitals.

The centralization of capitals or the process of their attraction becomes more intense, in proportion as the specifically capitalist mode of production develops along with accumulation. In its turn, centralization becomes one of the greatest levers of this development. It shortens and quickens the transformation of separate processes of production into processes socially combined and carried out on a large scale.

The increasing bulk of individual masses of capital becomes the material basis of an uninterrupted revolution in the mode of production itself. Continually the capitalist mode of production conquers branches of industry not yet wholly, or only sporadically, or only formally, subjugated by it. At the same time there grow up on its soil new branches of industry, such as could not exist without it. Finally, in the branches of industry already carried on upon the capitalist basis, the productiveness of labor is made to ripen, as if in a hothouse. In all these cases, the number of laborers falls in proportion to the mass of the means of production worked up by them. An ever increasing part of the capital is turned into means of production, an ever decreasing one into labor-power. With the extent, the concentration and the technical efficiency of the means of production, the degree lessens progressively, in which the latter are means of employment for laborers. A steam plow is an incomparably more efficient means of production than an ordinary plow, but the capital-value laid out in it is an incomparably smaller means for employing men than if it were laid out in ordinary plows. At first, it is the mere adding of new capital to old, which allows of the expansion and technical revolution of the material conditions of the process of production. But soon the change of composition and the technical transformation get more or less completely hold of all old capital that has reached the term of its reproduction, and therefore has to be replaced. This metamorphosis of old capital is independent, to a certain extent, of the absolute growth of social capital, in the same way as its centralization. But this centralization which only redistributes the social capital already to hand, and melts into one a number of old capitals, works in its turn as a powerful agent in this metamorphosis of old capital.

On the one hand, therefore, the additional capital formed in the course of accumulation attracts fewer and fewer laborers in proportion to its magnitude. On the other hand, the old capital periodically reproduced with change of composition, repels more and more of the laborers formerly employed by it.

Section 3.—PROGRESSIVE PRODUCTION OF A RELATIVE SURPLUS POPULATION OR INDUSTRIAL RESERVE ARMY.

The accumulation of capital, though originally appearing as its quantitative extension only, is effected, as we have seen, under a progressive qualitative change in its composition, under a constant increase of its constant, at the expense of its variable constituent.

The specifically capitalist mode of production, the development of the productive power of labor corresponding to it, and the change thence resulting in the organic composition of capital, do not merely keep pace with the advance of accumulation, or with the growth of social wealth. They develop at a much quicker rate, because mere accumulation, the absolute increase of the total social capital, is accompanied by the centralization of the individual capitals of which that total is made up; and because the change in the technological composition of the additional capital goes hand in hand with a similar change in the technological composition of the original capital. With the advance of accumulation, therefore, the proportion of constant to variable capital changes. If it was originally say 1:1, it now becomes successively 2:1, 3:1, 4:1, 5:1, 7:1, &c., so that, as the capital increases, instead of $\frac{1}{2}$ of its total value, only $\frac{1}{3}$, $\frac{1}{4}$, $\frac{1}{5}$, $\frac{1}{6}$, $\frac{1}{8}$, &c., is transformed into labor-power, and, on the other hand, $\frac{2}{3}$, $\frac{3}{4}$, $\frac{4}{5}$, $\frac{5}{6}$, $\frac{7}{8}$ into means of production. Since the demand for labor is determined not by the amount of capital as a whole, but by its variable constituent alone, that demand falls progressively with the increase of the total capital, instead of, as previously assumed, rising in proportion to it. It falls relatively to the magnitude of the total capital, and at an accelerated rate, as this magnitude increases. With the growth of the total capital, its variable constituent or the labor incorporated in it, also does increase, but in a constantly diminishing proportion. The intermediate pauses are shortened, in which accumulation works as simple extension of production, on a given technical basis. It is not merely that an accelerated accumulation of total capital, accelerated in a constantly growing progression, is needed to absorb an additional number of laborers, or even, on account of the constant metamorphosis of old capital, to keep employed those already functioning. In its turn, this increasing accumulation and centralization becomes a source of new changes in the composition of capital, of a more accelerated diminution of its variable, as compared with its constant constituent. This accelerated relative diminution of the variable constituent, that goes along with the accelerated increase of the total capital, and moves more rapidly than this increase, takes the inverse form. at the other pole, of an apparently absolute increase of the laboring population, an increase always moving more rapidly than that of the variable capital or the means of employment. But in fact, it is capitalistic accumulation itself that constantly produces, and produces in the direct ratio of its own energy and extent, a relatively redundant population of laborers, *i.e.*, a population of greater extent than suffices for the average needs of the self-expansion of capital, and therefore a surplus population.

Considering the social capital in its totality, the movement of its accumulation now causes periodical changes, affecting it more or less as a whole, now distributes its various phases simultaneously over the different spheres of production. In some spheres a change in the composition of capital occurs without increase of its absolute magnitude, as a consequence of simple centralization; in others the absolute growth of capital is connected with absolute diminution of its variable constituent, or of the labor-power absorbed by it; in others again, capital continues growing for a time on its given technical basis, and attracts additional labor-power in proportion to its increase, while at other times it undergoes organic change, and lessens its variable constituent; in all spheres, the increase of the variable part of capital, and therefore of the number of laborers employed by it, is always connected with violent fluctuations and transitory pròduction of surplus-population, whether this takes the more striking form of the repulsion of laborers already employed, or the less evident but not less real form of the more difficult absorption of the additional laboring population through the usual channels. With the magnitude of social capital already functioning, and the degree of its increase, with the extension of the scale of production, and the mass of the laborers set in motion, with the development of the productiveness of their labor, with the greater breadth and fullness of all sources of wealth, there is also an extension of the scale on which greater attraction of laborers by capital is accompanied by their greater repulsion; the rapidity of the change in the organic composition of capital, and in its technical form increases, and an increasing number of spheres of production becomes involved in this change, now simultaneously, now alternately. The laboring population therefore produces, along with the accumulation of capital produced by it, the means by which itself is made relatively superfluous, is turned into a relative surplus population; and it does this to an always increasing extent. This is a law of population peculiar to the capitalist mode of production; and in fact every special historic mode of production has its own special laws of population, historically valid within its limits alone. An abstract law of population exists for plants and animals only, and only insofar as man has not interfered with them.

But if a surplus laboring population is a necessary product of accumulation or of the development of wealth on a capitalist basis, this surplus population becomes, conversely, the lever of capitalistic accumulation, nay, a condition of existence of the capitalist mode of production. It forms a disposable industrial reserve army, that belongs to capital quite as absolutely as if the latter had bred it at its own cost. Independently of the limits of the actual increase of population, it creates, for the changing needs of the self-expansion of capital, a mass of human material always ready for exploitation. With accumulation, and the development of the productiveness of labor that accompanies it, the power of sudden expansion of capital grows also; it grows, not merely because the elasticity of the capital already functioning increases, not merely because the absolute wealth of society expands, of which capital only forms an elastic part, not merely because credit, under every special stimulus, at once places an unusual part of this wealth at the disposal of production in the form of additional capital; it grows, also, because the technical conditions of the process of production themselves—machinery, means of transport, &c.—now admit of the rapidest transformation of masses of surplus product into additional means of production. The mass of social wealth, overflowing with the advance of accumulation, and transformable into additional capital, thrusts itself frantically into old branches of production, whose market suddenly expands, or into newly formed branches,

such as railways, &c., the need for which grows out of the
development of the old ones. In all such cases, there must
be the possibility of throwing great masses of men suddenly on the decisive points without injury to the scale
of production in other spheres. Overpopulation supplies
these masses. The course characteristic of modern industry, *viz.*, a decennial cycle (interrupted by smaller oscillations) of periods of average activity, production at high
pressure, crisis and stagnation, depends on the constant
formation, the greater or less absorption, and the reforma-
tion of the industrial reserve army of surplus population.
In their turn, the varying phases of the industrial cycle
recruit the surplus population, and become one of the
most energetic agents of its reproduction. This peculiar
course of modern industry, which occurs in no earlier
period of human history, was also impossible in the child-
hood of capitalist production. The composition of capital
changed, but very slowly. With its accumulation, therefore, there kept pace, on the whole, a corresponding
growth in the demand for labor. Slow as was the advance
of accumulation compared with that of more modern
times, it found a check in the natural limits of the exploitable laboring population, limits which could only be
got rid of by forcible means to be mentioned later. The
expansion by fits and starts of the scale of production is
the preliminary to its equally sudden contraction; the
latter again evokes the former, but the former is impossible without disposable human material, without an increase in the number of laborers independently of the
absolute growth of the population. This increase is effected
by the simple process that constantly "sets free" a part
of the laborers; by methods which lessen the number of
laborers employed in proportion to the increased production. The whole form of the movement of modern industry
depends, therefore, upon the constant transformation of
a part of the laboring population into unemployed or half-
employed hands. The superficiality of political economy
shows itself in the fact that it looks upon the expansion
and contraction of credit, which is a mere symptom of the
periodic changes of the industrial cycle, as their cause.

As the heavenly bodies, once thrown into a certain definite motion, always repeat this, so is it with social production as soon as it is once thrown into this movement of alternate expansion and contraction. Effects, in their turn, become causes, and the varying accidents of the whole process, which always reproduces its own conditions, take on the form of periodicity. When this periodicity is once consolidated, even political economy then sees that the production of a relative surplus population—*i.e.*, surplus with regard to the average needs of the self-expansion of capital—is a necessary condition of modern industry. . . .

Up to this point it has been assumed that the increase or diminution of the variable capital corresponds rigidly with the increase or diminution of the number of laborers employed.

The number of laborers commanded by capital may remain the same, or even fall, while the variable capital increases. This is the case if the individual laborer yields more labor, and therefore his wages increase and this although the price of labor remains the same or even falls, only more slowly than the mass of labor rises. Increase of variable capital, in this case, becomes an index of more labor, but not of more laborers employed. It is the absolute interest of every capitalist to press a given quantity of labor out of a smaller, rather than a greater number of laborers, if the cost is about the same. In the latter case, the outlay of constant capital increases in proportion to the mass of labor set in action; in the former that increase is much smaller. The more extended the scale of production, the stronger this motive. Its force increases with the accumulation of capital.

We have seen that the development of the capitalist mode of production and of the productive power of labor —at once the cause and effect of accumulation—enables the capitalist, with the same outlay of variable capital, to set in action more labor by greater exploitation (extensive or intensive) of each individual labor-power. We have further seen that the capitalist buys with the same capital a greater mass of labor-power, as he progressively replaces skilled laborers by less skilled, mature labor-power by immature, male by female, that of adults by that of young persons or children.

On the one hand, therefore, with the progress of accumulation, a larger variable capital sets more labor in action without enlisting more laborers; on the other, a variable capital of the same magnitude sets in action more labor with the same mass of labor-power; and, finally, a greater number of inferior labor-power by displacement of higher.

The production of a relative surplus population, or the setting free of laborers, goes on therefore yet more rapidly than the technical revolution of the process of production that accompanies, and is accelerated by, the advances of accumulation; and more rapidly than the corresponding diminution of the variable part of capital as compared with the constant. If the means of production, as they increase in extent and effective power, become to a less extent means of employment of laborers, this state of things is again modified by the fact that in proportion as the productiveness of labor increases, capital increases its supply of labor more quickly than its demand for laborers. The overwork of the employed part of the working class swells the ranks of the reserve, while conversely the greater pressure that the latter by its competition exerts on the former, forces these to submit to overwork and to subjugation under the dictates of capital. The condemnation of one part of the working class to enforced idleness by the overwork of the other part, and the converse, becomes a means of enriching the individual capitalists, and accelerates at the same time the production of the industrial reserve army on a scale corresponding with the advance of social accumulation. How important is this element in the formation of the relative surplus population, is shown by the example of England. Her technical means for saving labor are colossal. Nevertheless, if tomorrow morning labor generally were reduced to a rational amount, and proportioned to the different sections of the working class according to age and sex, the working population to hand would be absolutely insufficient for the carrying on of national production on its present scale.

The great majority of the laborers now "unproductive" would have to be turned into "productive" ones.

Taking them as a whole, the general movements of wages are exclusively regulated by the expansion and contraction of the industrial reserve army, and these again correspond to the periodic changes of the industrial cycle. They are, therefore, not determined by the variations of the absolute number of the working population, but by the varying proportions in which the working class is divided into active and reserve army, by the increase or diminution in the relative amount of the surplus population, by the extent to which it is now absorbed, now set free. For modern industry with its decennial cycles and periodic phases, which, moreover, as accumulation advances, are complicated by irregular oscillations following each other more and more quickly, that would indeed be a beautiful law, which pretends to make the action of capital dependent on the absolute variation of the population, instead of regulating the demand and supply of labor by the alternate expansion and contraction of capital, the labor-market now appearing relatively underfull, because capital is expanding, now again overfull, because it is contracting. Yet this is the dogma of the economists. According to them, wages rise in consequence of accumulation of capital. The higher wages stimulate the working population to more rapid multiplication, and this goes on until the labor-market becomes too full, and therefore capital, relatively to the supply of labor, becomes insufficient. Wages fall, and now we have the reverse of the medal. The working population is little by little decimated as the result of the fall in wages, so that capital is again in excess relatively to them, or, as others explain it, falling wages and the corresponding increase in the exploitation of the laborer again accelerates accumulation, while, at the same time, the lower wages hold the increase of the working class in check. Then comes again the time, when the supply of labor is less than the demand, wages rise, and so on. A beautiful mode of motion this for developed capitalist production! Before, in consequence of the rise of wages, any positive increase of the population really

fit for work could occur, the time would have been passed
again and again, during which the industrial campaign
must have been carried through, the battle fought and
won. . . .

The industrial reserve army, during the periods of
stagnation and average prosperity, weighs down the active labor-army; during the periods of overproduction
and paroxysm, it holds its pretensions in check. Relative
surplus population is therefore the pivot upon which the
law of demand and supply of labor works. It confines the
field of action of this law within the limits absolutely
convenient to the activity of exploitation and to the domination of capital.

This is the place to return to one of the grand exploits
of economic apologetics. It will be remembered that if
through the introduction of new, or the extension of old,
machinery, a portion of variable capital is transformed into
constant, the economic apologist interprets this operation
which "fixes" capital and by that very act sets laborers
"free," in exactly the opposite way, pretending that it
sets free capital for the laborers. Only now can one fully
understand the effrontery of these apologists. What are
set free are not only the laborers immediately turned out
by the machines, but also their future substitutes in the
rising generation, and the additional contingent, that with
the usual extension of trade on the old basis would be
regularly absorbed. They are now all "set free," and every
new bit of capital looking out for employment can dispose
of them. Whether it attracts them or others, the effect on
the general labor demand will be nil, if this capital is
just sufficient to take out of the market as many laborers
as the machines threw upon it. If it employs a smaller
number, that of the supernumeraries increases; if it employs a greater, the general demand for labor only increases to the extent of the excess of the employed over
those "set free." The impulse that additional capital, seek-
ing an outlet, would otherwise have given to the general
demand for labor, is therefore in every case neutral-
ized to the extent of the laborers thrown out of employment by the machine. That is to say, the mecha-

nism of capitalistic production so manages matters that the absolute increase of capital is accompanied by no corresponding rise in the general demand for labor. And this the apologist calls a compensation for the misery, the sufferings, the possible death of the displaced laborers during the transition period that banishes them into the industrial reserve army! The demand for labor is not identical with increase of capital, nor supply of labor with increase of the working class. It is not a case of two independent forces working on one another. *Les dés sont pipés.*[5] Capital works on both sides at the same time. If its accumulation, on the one hand, increases the demand for labor, it increases on the other the supply of laborers by the "setting free" of them, while at the same time the pressure of the unemployed compels those that are employed to furnish more labor, and therefore makes the supply of labor, to a certain extent, independent of the supply of laborers. The action of the law of supply and demand of labor on this basis completes the despotism of capital. As soon, therefore, as the laborers learn the secret, how it comes to pass that in the same measure as they work more, as they produce more wealth for others, and as the productive power of their labor increases, so in the same measure even their function as a means of the self-expansion of capital becomes more and more precarious for them; as soon as they discover that the degree of intensity of the competition among themselves depends wholly on the pressure of the relative surplus population; as soon as, by Trades' Unions, &c., they try to organize a regular co-operation between employed and unemployed in order to destroy or to weaken the ruinous effects of this natural law of capitalistic production on their class, so soon capital and its sycophant, political economy, cry out at the infringement of the "eternal" and so to say "sacred" law of supply and demand. Every combination of employed and unemployed disturbs the "harmonious" action of this law. But, on the other hand, as soon as (in the colonies, *e.g.*,) adverse circumstances prevent the creation of an industrial reserve army and, with it, the absolute

[5] **Les dés sont pipés,** The dice are loaded

dependence of the working class upon the capitalist class, capital, along with its commonplace Sancho Panza, rebels against the "sacred" law of supply and demand, and tries to check its inconvenient action by forcible means and state interference.

Section 4.—DIFFERENT FORMS OF THE RELATIVE SURPLUS POPULATION. THE GENERAL LAW OF CAPITALISTIC AC-CUMULATION.

The relative surplus population exists in every possible form. Every laborer belongs to it during the time when he is only partially employed or wholly unemployed. Not taking into account the great periodically recurring forms that the changing phases of the industrial cycle impress on it, now an acute form during the crisis, then again a chronic form during dull times—it has always three forms, the floating, the latent, the stagnant.

In the centers of modern industry—factories, manufacturers, ironworks, mines, &c.—the laborers are sometimes repelled, sometimes attracted again in greater masses, the number of those employed increasing on the whole, although in a constantly decreasing proportion to the scale of production. Here the surplus population exists in the floating form.

In the automatic factories, as in all the great workshops, where machinery enters as a factor, or where only the modern divisions of labor is carried out, large numbers of boys are employed up to the age of maturity. When this term is once reached, only a very small number continue to find employment in the same branches of industry, while the majority are regularly discharged. This majority forms an element of the floating surplus population, growing with the extension of those branches of industry. Part of them emigrates, following in fact capital that has emigrated. One consequence is that the female population grows more rapidly than the male, *teste* England. That the natural increase of the number of laborers does not satisfy the requirements of the accumulation of capital, and yet all the time is in excess of them, is a contradiction inherent to the movement of capital itself. It wants larger numbers of youthful laborers, a smaller number of adults. The contradiction is not more glaring than that other one that there is a complaint of the want of hands, while at the same time many thousands are out of work, because the division of labor chains them to a particular branch of industry.

The consumption of labor-power by capital is, besides, so rapid that the laborer, halfway through his life, has already more or less completely lived himself out. He falls into the ranks of the supernumeraries, or is thrust down from a higher to a lower step in the scale. It is precisely among the work-people of modern industry that we meet with the shortest duration of life. Dr. Lee, Medical Officer of Health for Manchester, stated "that the average age at death of the Manchester . . . upper middle class was 38 years, while the average age at death of the laboring class was 17; while at Liverpool those figures were represented as 35 against 15. It thus appeared that the well-to-do classes had a lease of life which was more than double the value of that which fell to the lot of the less favored citizens." [1] In order to conform to these circumstances, the absolute increase of this section of the proletariat must take places under conditions that shall swell their numbers, although the individual elements are used up rapidly. Hence, rapid renewal of the generations of laborers (this law does not hold for the other classes of the population). This social need is met by early marriages, a necessary consequence of the conditions in which the laborers of modern industry live, and by the premium that the exploitation of children sets on their production.

As soon as capitalist production takes possession of agriculture, and in proportion to the extent to which it does so, the demand for an agricultural laboring population falls absolutely, while the accumulation of the capital em-

[1] [Note by Marx] Opening address to the Sanitary Conference, Birmingham, January 15th, 1875, by J. Chamberlain, Mayor of the town, now (1883) President of the Board of Trade

ployed in agriculture advances, without this repulsion being, as in nonagricultural industries, compensated by a greater attraction. Part of the agricultural population is therefore constantly on the point of passing over into an urban or manufacturing proletariat, and on the look-out for circumstances favorable to this transformation. (Manufacture is used here in the sense of all nonagricultural industries.) This source of relative surplus population is thus constantly flowing. But the constant flow towards the towns presupposes, in the country itself, a constant latent surplus population, the extent of which becomes evident only when its channels of outlet open to exceptional width. The agricultural laborer is therefore reduced to the minimum of wages, and always stands with one foot already in the swamp of pauperism.

The third category of the relative surplus population, the stagnant, forms a part of the active labor army, but with extremely irregular employment. Hence it furnishes to capital an inexhaustible reservoir of disposable labor-power. Its conditions of life sink below the average normal level of the working class; this makes it at once the broad basis of special branches of capitalist exploitation. It is characterized by maximum of working time, and minimum of wages. We have learned to know its chief form under the rubric of "domestic industry." It recruits itself constantly from the supernumerary forces of modern industry and agriculture, and specially from those decaying branches of industry where handicraft is yielding to manufacture, manufacture to machinery. Its extent grows, as with the extent and energy of accumulation, the creation of a surplus population advances. But it forms at the same time a self-reproducing and self-perpetuating element of the working class, taking a proportionally greater part in the general increase of that class than the other elements. In fact, not only the number of births and deaths, but the absolute size of the families stand in inverse proportion to the height of wages, and therefore to the amount of means of subsistence of which the different categories of laborers dispose. This law of capitalistic society would sound absurd to savages, or even civilized colonists. It calls to mind the boundless reproduction of animals individually weak and constantly hunted down.[2]

The lowest sediment of the relative surplus population finally dwells in the sphere of pauperism. Exclusive of vagabonds, criminals, prostitutes, in a word, the "dangerous" classes, this layer of society consists of three categories. First, those able to work. One need only glance superficially at the statistics of English pauperism to find that the quantity of paupers increases with every crisis, and diminishes with every revival of trade. Second, orphans and pauper children. These are candidates for the industrial reserve-army, and are, in times of great prosperity, as 1860, *e.g.*, speedily and in large numbers enrolled in the active army of laborers. Third, the demoralized and ragged, and those unable to work, chiefly people who succumb to their incapacity for adaptation, due to the division of labor; people who have passed the normal age of the laborer; the victims of industry, whose number increases with the increase of dangerous machinery, of mines, chemical works, &c., the mutilated, the sickly, the widows, &c. Pauperism is the hospital of the active labor-army and the dead weight of the industrial reserve-army. Its production is included in that of the relative surplus population, its necessity in theirs; along with the surplus population, pauperism forms a condition of capitalist production, and of the capitalist development of wealth. It enters into the *faux frais*[3] of capitalist production; but capital knows how to throw these, for the most

---

[2] [Note by Marx] "Poverty seems favourable to generation." (A. Smith.) This is even a specially wise arrangement of God, according to the gallant and witty Abbé Galiani. "Thus it comes to pass that the men who practice occupations of primary utility breed abundantly." F. Galiani, *Della Moneta* (Custodi's edn., Milan, 1803). "Misery up to the extreme point of famine and pestilence, instead of checking, tends to increase population." S. Laing, *National Distress* (London, 1844), p. 69. After Laing has illustrated this by statistics, he continues: "If the people were all in easy circumstances, the world would soon be depopulated."

[3] **faux frais**, incidental expenses

part, from its own shoulders on to those of the working class and the lower middle class.

The greater the social wealth, the functioning capital, the extent and energy of its growth, and, therefore, also the absolute mass of the proletariat and the productiveness of its labor, the greater is the industrial reserve-army. The same causes which develop the expansive power of capital, develops also the labor-power at its disposal. The relative mass of the industrial reserve-army increases therefore with the potential energy of wealth. But the greater this reserve-army in proportion to the active labor-army, the greater is the mass of a consolidated surplus population, whose misery is in inverse ratio to its torment of labor. The more extensive, finally, the Lazarus-layers of the working-class, and the industrial reserve-army, the greater is official pauperism. *This is the absolute general law of capitalist accumulation.* Like all other laws it is modified in its working by many circumstances, the analysis of which does not concern us here.

The folly is now patent of the economic wisdom that preaches to the laborers the accommodation of their number to the requirements of capital. The mechanism of capitalist production and accumulation constantly effects this adjustment. The first word of this adaptation is the creation of a relative surplus population, or industrial reserve-army. Its last word is the misery of constantly extending strata of the active army of labor, and the dead weight of pauperism.

The law by which a constantly increasing quantity of means of production, thanks to the advance in the productiveness of social labor, may be set in movement by a progressively diminishing expenditure of human power, this law, in a capitalist society—where the laborer does not employ the means of production, but the means of production employ the laborer—undergoes a complete inversion and is expressed thus: the higher the productiveness of labor, the greater is the pressure of the laborers on the means of employment, the more precarious, therefore, becomes their condition of existence, viz., the sale of their own labor-power for the increasing of another's wealth, or for the self-expansion of capital. The fact that the means of production, and the productiveness of labor, increase more rapidly than the productive population, expresses itself, therefore, capitalistically in the inverse form that the laboring population always increases more rapidly than the conditions under which capital can employ this increase for its own self-expansion.

We saw in Part IV, when analysing the production of relative surplus value: within the capitalist system all methods for raising the social productiveness of labor are brought about at the cost of the individual laborer; all means for the development of production transform themselves into means of domination over, and exploitation of, the producers; they mutilate the laborer into a fragment of a man, degrade him to the level of an appendage of a machine, destroy every remnant of charm in his work and turn it into a hated toil; they estrange from him the intellectual potentialities of the labor-process in the same proportion as science is incorporated in it as an independent power; they distort the conditions under which he works, subject him during the labor-process to a despotism the more hateful for its meanness; they transform his lifetime into working time, and drag his wife and child beneath the wheels of the juggernaut of capital. But all methods for the production of surplus value are at the same time methods of accumulation; and every extension of accumulation becomes again a means for the development of those methods. It follows therefore that in proportion as capital accumulates, the lot of the laborer, be his payment high or low, must grow worse. The law, finally, that always equilibrates the relative surplus population, or industrial reserve-army, to the extent and energy of accumulation, this law rivets the laborer to capital more firmly than the wedges of Vulcan did Prometheus to the rock. It establishes an accumulation of misery, corresponding with accumulation of capital. Accumulation of wealth at one pole is, therefore, at the same time accumulation of misery, agony of toil, slavery, ignorance, brutality, mental degradation, at the opposite pole, i.e., on the side of the class that produces its own product in the form of capital.

BIBLIOGRAPHY

BIOGRAPHIES

Franz Mehring, *Karl Marx: The Story of his Life*. Translated E. Fitzgerald (London, 1936 and 1948).

Isaiah Berlin, *Karl Marx: His Life and Environment*. Home University Library (London, 1939 and 1948).

E. H. Carr, *Karl Marx: A Study in Fanaticism* (London, 1935).

Gustav Mayer, *Friedrich Engels* (London, 1935).

PRINCIPAL WORKS OF MARX AND ENGELS IN ENGLISH

Karl Marx: Selected Works. 2 vols. Prepared by the Marx-Engels-Lenin Institute, Moscow, under the editorship of V. Adoratsky. English edition by C. P. Dutt (Lawrence and Wishart, London, 1942).

Selected Correspondence of Marx and Engels, 1846-1895 (New York, 1934).

Marx, *The Poverty of Philosophy* (New York, 1936).

The Class Struggles in France, 1848-50 (London, 1934).

The Eighteenth Brumaire of Louis Bonaparte (London, 1935).

The Civil War in France (London, 1933).

A Contribution to the Critique of Political Economy (Chicago, 1904).

Capital. Volume I, Translated by Moore and Aveling and revised by E. Untermann (Chicago, 1906). Reimpression as Modern Library Giant (New York, n.d.).

Volume I. Translated by E. and C. Paul (London, 1928). Everyman Library edn. (London, 1930).

Vols. II and III. Translated by E. Untermann (Chicago, 1907).

Critique of the Gotha Programme (New York, 1933 and Moscow, 1947).

Marx and Engels, *The German Ideology* (New York, 1947).

The Communist Manifesto. Many edns.

Germany: Revolution and Counter-Revolution (London, 1933).

Engels, *Herr Eugen Duehring's Revolution in Science* (London, 1935).

Origin of the Family, Private Property and the State (London, 1940).

CRITICISM

M. M. Bober, *Karl Marx' Interpretation of History* (Cambridge, Mass., 1927 and 1948).

E. von Boehm-Bawerk, *Karl Marx and the Close of His System.* Paul M. Sweezy (ed.) (New York, 1949).

S. H. Chang, *The Marxian Theory of the State* (Philadelphia, 1931).

Alexander Gray, *The Socialist Tradition from Moses to Lenin* (London, 1946).

George Lichtheim, *Marxism: An Historical and Critical Study* (New York, 1961).

K. R. Popper, *The Open Society and Its Enemies* (Princeton, 1950).

J. Schumpeter, *Capitalism, Socialism and Democracy* (London, 1943).

Paul M. Sweezy, *The Theory of Capitalist Development* (New York, 1942 and 1946).

Robert C. Tucker, *Philosophy and Myth in Karl Marx* (Cambridge, England, 1961).

Adam B. Ulam, *The Unfinished Revolution: An Essay on the Sources of Influence of Marxism and Communism* (New York, 1960).

V. Venables, *Human Nature: the Marxian View* (New York, 1945).